S. Hrg. 113–112

PRESERVING THE RIGHTS OF SERVICEMEMBERS, VETERANS, AND THEIR FAMILIES IN THE FINANCIAL MARKETPLACE

HEARING

BEFORE THE

COMMITTEE ON VETERANS' AFFAIRS
UNITED STATES SENATE

ONE HUNDRED THIRTEENTH CONGRESS

FIRST SESSION

JULY 31, 2013

Printed for the use of the Committee on Veterans' Affairs

Available via the World Wide Web: http://www.fdsys.gov

U.S. GOVERNMENT PRINTING OFFICE

82–715 PDF   WASHINGTON : 2014

For sale by the Superintendent of Documents, U.S. Government Printing Office
Internet: bookstore.gpo.gov   Phone: toll free (866) 512–1800; DC area (202) 512–1800
Fax: (202) 512–2104   Mail: Stop IDCC, Washington, DC 20402–0001

CONTENTS

JULY 31, 2013

SENATORS

WITNESSES

PRESERVING THE RIGHTS OF SERVICEMEMBERS, VETERANS, AND THEIR FAMILIES IN THE FINANCIAL MARKETPLACE

WEDNESDAY, JULY 31, 2013

U.S. SENATE,
COMMITTEE ON VETERANS' AFFAIRS,
Washington, DC.

The Committee met, pursuant to notice, at 9:55 a.m., in room SR–418, Russell Senate Office Building, Hon. Bernard Sanders, Chairman of the Committee, presiding.

Present: Senators Sanders, Hirono, and Boozman.

OPENING STATEMENT OF HON. BERNARD SANDERS, CHAIRMAN, U.S. SENATOR FROM VERMONT

Chairman SANDERS. The hearing will come to order a little bit early because we have got votes at 10:45 and then the President is coming to a caucus later and that I am going to have to attend.

I want to thank all of our panelists and everyone with us today. Senator Boozman and other Senators will be joining us for the discussion of an issue that many of us feel very strongly about.

As everyone knows, we passed important legislation which essentially says that when men and women go off to war they are not going to get ripped off at home, not by financial institutions and not by people trying to take advantage of benefits which they have earned. I can tell you firsthand, as you all know, people go off to war, families are left with kids, they are struggling back home, they are vulnerable, and we are not going to allow those people to be taken advantage of.

The panelists that we have here today have done a wonderful job in trying to protect those servicemembers and we are going to hear from them in a moment.

I remain deeply troubled by the violations of the SCRA that occurred within the mortgage lending industry within the past few years. In a 2012 report, the GAO identified over 14,000 instances of financial institutions failing to properly reduce servicemembers' mortgage interest rates, as the law provides, and over 300 improper foreclosures.

These violations are completely unacceptable. Unfortunately, the challenges faced by our servicemembers do not end there. The Consumer Financial Protection Bureau has identified similar practices and concerns within the student loan servicing market. This unacceptable behavior also must end. We must continue to improve education about the protections of the SCRA, industry must improve its compliance with the Act, and finally, aggressive enforcement of these protections must continue when violations occur.

I think we are all in agreement that when men and women put their lives on the line defending our country, they should not be subjected to the types of behavior we have seen in the past. that is why today's discussion about how we can continue to improve and enhance the SCRA is so terribly important.

I am going to end my remarks at this point. Senator Boozman, I want to give the mic over to you and then I would like us to hear from the panel.

STATEMENT OF HON. JOHN BOOZMAN,
U.S. SENATOR FROM ARKANSAS

Senator BOOZMAN. Yes, sir, I want to agree and I want to thank you and Ranking Member Burr for making it so that we can have this very, very important hearing. In the interest of time—because we have votes not too far from now, and also I know the President is coming over—so I am going to put my statement in the record.

Briefly, I agree with you so much in the sense this is so important. Servicemembers—my dad did 20 years in the Air Force. This is a family affair and it is difficult. It is a unique situation. Families are separated, especially with the op temp (operating temperature) that we have going on right now, taking care of finances, you know, those discussions that most of us in everyday life take for granted is simply much more difficult in that situation.

So, we do want to protect our servicemembers. We want to make sure that they are treated right. They have got enough to deal with without unscrupulous predators preying on them. So, again, thank you for being here, and with your permission, I will put my statement in the record, Mr. Chairman.

Chairman SANDERS. Absolutely. And thank you very much, Senator Boozman.

[The prepared statement of Senator Boozman follows:]

PREPARED STATEMENT OF HON. JOHN BOOZMAN,
U.S. SENATOR FROM ARKANSAS

Mr. Chairman, thank you for holding this hearing today. And thank you to all of our witnesses and Members of the Committee who share the universal principle that our active duty servicemembers and their families should have the tools they need to make sound financial decisions and adequate protections from abusive financial practices.

From the ongoing efforts and the testimony before us today, it is clear that there continues to be a strong public private partnership to serve every member of the military.

Whether it is legal protections from foreclosure during military service, caps on loan interest rates, and laws that discourage predatory lending, or initiatives to increase financial literacy among servicemembers and private sector initiatives to better serve our military personnel—there are rigorous ongoing efforts to ensure that our servicemembers are able to balance the challenges that accompany military service, as well as the financial strains that most working class families in America deal with every day.

At the same time, military service is unique and the financial strains military families face—because they choose to serve our Nation in uniform—can often be more stressful than those experienced by civilian families. Furthermore, the range of benefits for financial services and economic opportunity can make them targets for those who seek to take advantage. It is therefore appropriate for us to have public and private mechanisms in place to protect them from predatory lenders and empower them to make the right decisions.

At the same time, as we seek to implement these programs, we must ensure that these programs empower servicemembers and do not restrict their economic freedom and options, whether it be in their choice of financial tools or how they choose to exercise the economic opportunity benefits that they have earned. Our military are selective, and every member of our military is able in mind and body. We all care so deeply for the wellbeing of our servicemembers and their families and I believe that everyone here wishes to serve them in good faith. At the same time, we should be cautious that we do not impose rules and regulations on servicemembers and the institutions that serve them which could inadvertently limit their choices and economic freedom. Just because bad actors have inappropriately and illegally sought to take advantage of the benefits for which these men and women have sacrificed so greatly, we shouldn't limit their options in our efforts to help them.

We should continue to focus on economic empowerment and focused programs that target those bad actors. We should improve financial literacy training for servicemembers, increase interagency cooperation of SCRA laws, and ensure that the programs we currently have are working effectively, and we should work with the financial industry and those who wish to be a part of the solution to enable better compliance with the law.

In closing, I look forward to this discussion today and am confident that it will lead us all in the direction of better serving and protecting servicemembers and their families, and improve our ability to conduct effective oversight of Federal agencies.

Thank you again Mr. Chairman for holding this hearing.

Chairman SANDERS. We are going to hear now from our very distinguished panel. First we will hear from Mrs. Holly Petraeus, Assistant Director, Office of Servicemember Affairs at the Consumer Financial Protection Bureau. Also with us is Colonel Paul Kantwill, Director of Legal Policy, Office of the Undersecretary for Personnel and Readiness of the Department of Defense. We will then hear from the final witness on this panel, Eric Halperin, Special Counsel for Fair Lending in the Civil Rights Division at the Department of Justice.

With that, Mrs. Petraeus, let us begin with you.

STATEMENT OF HOLLISTER K. PETRAEUS, ASSISTANT DIRECTOR, OFFICE OF SERVICEMEMBER AFFAIRS, CONSUMER FINANCIAL PROTECTION BUREAU

Ms. PETRAEUS. Chairman Sanders, Ranking Member Boozman, thank you for the opportunity to speak with you today. The Office of Servicemember Affairs, or OSA, as we call it at the CFPB, has three missions: to educate and empower servicemembers and their families to make better informed consumer decisions; to monitor military complaints to the Bureau and the responses to those complaints; and to coordinate with Federal and State agencies on consumer protection measures for the military.

Concerning our education mission, my team worked with DOD to create the financial module for their Transition Assistance Program, or TAP. We are also working on an initiative to offer financial coaching services to recently transitioned veterans.

As for complaints, in the last 2 years, the Bureau received approximately 4,500 complaints from veterans and their family members. About 49 percent of those complaints concerned mortgages, followed by 18 percent credit cards, 13 percent bank account servicing issues, and 8 percent credit reporting issues.

We have helped veterans who complained to us secure hundreds of thousands of dollars in monetary relief, as well as non-monetary relief. For example, a vet from North Carolina had a bank fee of nearly $2,000 that should have been waived because he was disabled. Within weeks of his filing a complaint with us, the bank removed the fee and refunded the interest charged.

As to coordinating with other Federal and State agencies, OSA has worked with Treasury and the Federal Housing Finance Agency on mortgage issues, with DOJ on SCRA issues, and with the VA on veterans issues, and obviously we talk all the time with DOD.

In the States, OSA has had great support from the Attorneys General, with 16 of them joining me at events in military communities, and from the State Directors of Veterans Affairs, and we work with the veteran service organizations, too. We have had a couple of town halls specifically for them.

I also did a telephone town hall last year with Senators Rockefeller and Manchin that reached thousands of veterans in West Virginia, and I have just added a veterans outreach specialist to my staff so we can do more.

In the last 2½ years, I have traveled to 28 States and about 60 military communities in the United States. One issue that has been raised consistently is aggressive marketing to veterans by certain institutions of higher education seeking those with G.I. Bill benefits. There is an extra incentive for for-profit colleges, in particular, to chase after military students because of the 90/10 proprietary college Federal funding cap. And I have heard of some very aggressive tactics to recruit them.

I spoke with a woman from the VA in Nevada who was overseeing vocational rehabilitation for vets. She told me that she had patients with Traumatic Brain Injury and PTSD who had been persuaded to sign up for college classes and did not even remember it. That did not stop the colleges from pressing them for full payment, even though they were not regularly attending classes.

Some schools were also pushing her patients to enroll in master's degree programs, though she believed they were not capable of doing the work. Their tactics were aggressive enough that she described it as, ''tormenting veterans.''

Another area of concern is that of financial institutions failing to provide SCRA protections to those who qualify for them, as you mentioned, and we do work with DOJ on these issues.

SCRA compliance problems are not limited to mortgage servicing. In the student loan servicing market, we have heard of lenders giving out incorrect or misleading information or even refusing to grant SCRA protections.

Another issue that I have heard about frequently concerns the veteran's benefit known as Aid and Attendance. Individuals and companies use it as a hook to sell their services to elderly veterans.

It may involve offering to help them qualify for Aid and Attendance, if they have too much money, by taking control of their assets and moving them into a trust where they cannot access them, as in a recent case in Washington State, or some retirement homes are now using the lure of Aid and Attendance to get veterans to move in on the premise that they will get the benefit and they will pay for everything. If the benefit is denied, this leaves the veteran in the position of being unable to afford to remain in the facility.

We have also seen a flood of advertising in the past year urging those with VA home loans to refinance. The Bureau and the FTC did a joint sweep of the ads which resulted in letters to a number of lenders concerning potential violations.

One last area of concern is pension advances. Offers to pay military retirees a lump sum in return for their future monthly retirement payments. These offers usually amount to pennies on the dollar and may be in violation of the law regarding assignment of pension benefits.

To conclude, the Office of Servicemember Affairs is working hard to fulfill its missions of education and consumer protection. Our veterans have done extraordinary service for our country and it is an honor for us at OSA to serve them and their families. Thank you for the opportunity to testify before the Committee.

[The prepared statement of Ms. Petraeus follows:]

PREPARED STATEMENT OF HOLLISTER K. PETRAEUS, ASSISTANT DIRECTOR, OFFICE OF SERVICEMEMBER AFFAIRS, CONSUMER FINANCIAL PROTECTION BUREAU

Chairman Sanders, Ranking Member Burr, and distinguished Members of the Committee, thank you for the opportunity to speak with you today about the Office of Servicemember Affairs at the Consumer Financial Protection Bureau (Bureau).

Many of you already know me as I've testified before you on other committees, and I've also had the opportunity to visit with some of you in your home States. But for those of you who are not familiar with my office, I'd like to take a few moments to tell you what we do.

As defined in the Dodd-Frank Act, the Office of Servicemember Affairs at the Bureau is responsible for:

• Developing and implementing initiatives to educate and empower servicemembers and their families to make better-informed decisions regarding consumer financial products and services;
• Monitoring military complaints about consumer financial products and services, including the Bureau and other Federal or State agency responses to those complaints; and
• Coordinating the efforts of Federal and State agencies regarding consumer protection measures relating to consumer financial products and services offered to, or used by, servicemembers and their families.

Concerning our education mission, in an effort that I think would be of interest to this Committee, my team worked with the Department of Defense (DOD) to create a financial module to be included in the recently revised Transition Assistance Program for those departing the military. And, in a logical follow-on, this year we're working on an initiative to offer financial coaching services to recently-transitioned veterans, to ensure they have some professional financial-planning support during the economically vulnerable time after they leave the service.

As for our complaint monitoring, from July 21, 2011 through July 6, 2013, the Bureau received approximately 4,516 complaints from veterans and their family members. The complaint volume from veterans has steadily increased over time, with 262 complaints received in 2011, 2,315 in 2012, and 1,939 complaints in the first six months of 2013. About 49 percent of the complaints from veterans have been mortgage complaints, followed by 18 percent credit card complaints, and 13 percent bank account or service complaints. We only started accepting complaints about credit-reporting companies in October 2012, but credit reporting is already the 4th highest complaint category for veterans at 8 percent, and is trending upward.

We have helped veterans who filed complaints secure hundreds of thousands of dollars in monetary relief. We've also assisted many others to obtain non-monetary relief, for example having errors on a credit report corrected, which helps them resolve problems that may have been affecting them for months or even years.

But these complaint statistics aren't just numbers to us: they represent military and veteran families and we know the impact consumer financial issues can have on their quality of life. In one complaint, a veteran from North Carolina was struggling with his bank for months over a fee of nearly $2,000 that should have been waived because he was disabled. Within weeks of his filing a complaint with the Bureau, the bank removed the fee and refunded the veteran for the interest that was charged in error. Although we can't promise specific results, I encourage servicemembers, veterans, retirees, and military spouses to go to consumerfinance.gov and file a complaint if they are having problems with a mortgage, credit card, student loan, or other consumer financial product. And I think it's fair to say that our Consumer Response team is making a real difference for many veterans and their families.

As to my office's third mission—coordinating with other Federal and State agencies—I have spent a significant amount of time doing just that. Our Office of Servicemember Affairs has worked with Federal agencies such as the Department of the Treasury and the Federal Housing Finance Agency on mortgage issues, with the Department of Justice (DOJ) on Servicemembers Civil Relief Act issues, and with the Department of Veterans Affairs (VA) concerning veterans' issues. And obviously my staff and I talk all the time with DOD.

In the States, I've had great support from the Attorneys General, with 16 of them personally joining me at events in military communities. In fact, on July 1st I was at MacDill Air Force Base in Florida at the invitation of Attorney General Pam Bondi to watch Governor Scott sign a bill to provide enhanced penalties for those who use deceptive or unfair trade practices in their dealings with servicemembers, veterans, and their families.

I've also had a very good relationship with the State Directors of Veterans Affairs, meeting with almost a dozen of them in their home States as well as addressing their national conference in May. And I work with the veterans' service organizations (VSOs), as well. I've done presentations to the Iraq and Afghanistan Veterans of America, the Vietnam Veterans of America, and the American Legion. We have also had a couple of town halls specifically for VSOs and intend to do more.

Speaking of town halls, I participated in a telephone town hall last year with Senator Manchin and Senator Rockefeller that reached thousands of veterans in the state of West Virginia, and I am eager to engage with veterans through initiatives such as these whenever I have the opportunity to do so. I should add that I have just added a veterans' outreach specialist to my staff so we can do more work on consumer protections and financial education for veterans.

Now, let me talk specifically about the issues that have come up during my travels to 28 States and about 60 military communities, where I have heard directly in the past two years from servicemembers, veterans, military retirees, and their families.

One issue that has been raised consistently throughout my travels is concern over aggressive marketing to military personnel, veterans, and their families by certain institutions of higher education seeking to attract individuals with access to GI Bill benefits. These institutions are pushing not only their educational programs, but also, in many cases, expensive private student loans to pay for the amount of tuition and fees not covered by the GI Bill.

There is an extra incentive for for-profit colleges, in particular, to chase after military students because of the 90–10 proprietary college Federal funding cap—a requirement that for-profit colleges get at least 10 percent of their revenue from sources other than Title IV Federal education funds administered by the Department of Education (ED). Military GI Bill and Tuition Assistance benefits are not Title IV funds, so they fall into the 10 percent category that these colleges need to fill—and we have heard of some very aggressive tactics to put GI Bill recipients into classes.

For example, a year ago when I was out in Nevada with Attorney General Catherine Cortez Masto, I spoke with a woman from the VA Regional Office there who was overseeing vocational rehabilitation for veterans. She told me that she had patients with Traumatic Brain Injury (TBI) and Post Traumatic Stress Disorder (PTSD) who had been persuaded to sign up for college classes, and didn't even remember doing so. That didn't stop the colleges from pressing them for full payment, even though they were not regularly attending classes. She said that some schools were also pushing her patients to enroll in Master's Degree programs even though she believed they were not capable of doing the work at that time. Their tactics were aggressive enough that she described it as "tormenting veterans." Obviously it distressed her to see her patients pressed to spend their GI Bill benefits in this manner.

On the same topic, in April 2012 I went to Fort Stewart, Georgia to watch the President sign an Executive Order 13607, "Establishing Principles of Excellence for Educational Institutions Serving Servicemembers, Veterans, Spouses, and Other Family Members." The Order directed the Departments of Defense, Veterans Affairs, and Education, in consultation with the Bureau and the Attorney General, to take steps to enable servicemembers, veterans and their families to get the information they need about the schools where they spend their education benefits. The Order also strengthened oversight and accountability within the Federal military and veterans' educational benefits programs.

I am pleased to report that there has been real progress since then, with DOD, ED, VA, DOJ, the Federal Trade Commission, and the Bureau working together to better protect and inform servicemembers, veterans, and military families about their education benefits. For example:

• The term ''GI Bill'' has now been trademarked by the VA;

• DOD has updated their rules to protect against aggressive commercial solicitation on military installations by educational institutions; and

• ED has finalized the ''Know Before You Owe Financial Aid Shopping Sheet,'' enabling veterans to make better-informed decisions about paying for college and choosing a school.

The State Attorneys General have been active, too, filing suit against certain colleges for deceptive marketing and aggressive recruiting tactics. And 19 of them joined Kentucky Attorney General Jack Conway in filing suit against a company called Quin Street that had a number of lead-generation Web sites marketing to GI Bill recipients. In addition to paying a monetary settlement and changing misleading content on their sites, Quin Street agreed as part of the settlement to give the URL www.gibill.com to the VA.

Certainly there is more work to be done, but I believe these and subsequent steps will help protect against some of the most egregious abuses we've seen in the past. That said, we intend to keep working with groups from the above agencies to see that the Order is implemented in a way that best serves our military and veterans.

Another area of concern that has arisen fairly frequently, both on my trips and via our complaint system, is that of financial institutions failing to provide Servicemembers Civil Relief Act (SCRA) protections to those who qualify for them. DOJ has explicit enforcement authority under SCRA, so we coordinate frequently with the DOJ Civil Rights Division and DOD concerning the SCRA-related components of the military complaints that we receive. In fact, my first testimony before Congress in this job was in February 2011 before the House Committee on Veterans' Affairs and the subject of the hearing was the failure of the largest banks to provide SCRA entitlements to their military customers—both the interest-rate reduction to six percent and foreclosure protection. I also had the opportunity to take part in a panel hosted by Senator Rockefeller and Congressman Elijah Cummings discussing the impact on military readiness when SCRA protections are violated.

Since then the State AGs, the Department of Housing and Urban Development (HUD) and DOJ have aggressively pursued this issue, resulting in a national mortgage settlement with the five largest mortgage lenders that was in part spurred by the lenders' failure to comply with the provisions of the SCRA. While I commend the settlement and their continued vigilance, we do continue to see compliance concerns in the complaints that military/veteran consumers file with the Bureau.

SCRA compliance problems are not limited to mortgage servicing; we've now identified other markets with similar problems. Most notably, in the student-loan servicing market, we've heard of lenders giving out incorrect or misleading information or even refusing to grant SCRA protections. Some examples:

• Servicemembers being told (incorrectly) that they must provide a letter from their commanding officer or ''certified'' orders in order to receive the interest-rate reduction to six percent;

• Officers being told to provide orders with an end date in order to receive the interest-rate reduction (officers' orders usually don't have end dates—they are indefinite);

• The lender terminating the interest-rate reduction at the end of one year because the servicemember does not provide proof of continuing active-duty service (proof that is not required under the SCRA);

• The lender placing the servicemember in forbearance automatically when SCRA rights are invoked, rather than simply providing the requested interest-rate reduction; and

• The lender failing to comply with a servicemember's request that the lender refund all the interest charged above 6 percent from the point of entry into active-duty military service. As long as the servicemember requests this SCRA protection within 180 days of leaving active duty, the lender must comply and issue a refund, no matter how long has passed since the servicemember entered active duty, even if it's been months or years.

We put out a report on this topic with the Bureau's Student Loan Ombudsman, along with an action guide for servicemembers. In the report we also raised concerns about an issue that arises when servicemembers attempt to replace older, pre-service student loans with a new Direct Consolidation Loan (to take advantage of Federal student loan repayment options such as Income-Based Repayment or Public Service Loan Forgiveness). Unfortunately, the law as currently written does not convey the "pre-service obligation" status of the old loans to the new Direct Loan, which has the unfortunate result of forcing some servicemembers to choose between the SCRA protection of a lower interest rate on their old loans or the prospect of income-based repayment and eventual loan forgiveness with a consolidated Direct Loan.

And although it is not an SCRA issue, while we're on the topic of student loans I wanted to raise a concern about veterans with private student loan debt who have been very severely injured during combat or at any time during their military service. It's a sad fact that some veterans with the most severe disabilities will never be capable of obtaining or performing a job that will enable them to repay that private student loan debt. However, as the law now stands, it is very difficult for them to discharge those debts despite the reality of their medical condition. It seems a shame that Federal student loans have such a provision for those with 100 percent disability, but there is currently no such relief for those who have private student loans.

Another issue that I have heard about frequently on my trips throughout the U.S. concerns abuses connected with the veterans' benefit known as Aid and Attendance, which I know this group is familiar with. I have heard from a number of State Veterans Affairs directors, starting with my trip to Montana at the invitation of Senator Tester in January 2012, that they are concerned about the increasing number of individuals and companies that use Aid and Attendance as a hook to sell their services to elderly veterans. I'd like to note a recent settlement by the Attorney General of Washington with three financial planning companies that were doing just that. These companies were offering help with obtaining Aid and Attendance but were requiring their customers to sign up for financial services first,—and then moving the veterans' assets into irrevocable trusts but not fully informing the veterans of the risks of doing so.

Aid and Attendance offers can take a variety of forms:

• It may be an offer from a lawyer or "veterans' advisor" to get the Aid and Attendance benefit for you—for a fee. In reality claims processing should be free, but in some cases veterans are being charged a "consultation fee" before the claim paperwork is begun.

• It may be a claim from a paid advisor that they can get the benefit for you more quickly than anyone else. But all VA benefits claims have to go through the standard VA evaluation process, and no one can bypass the system to get your claim approved faster than usual.

• It may involve offering to help you qualify for Aid and Attendance, if you have too much money, by taking control of your assets and moving them into a trust where you can't access them, as in the case in Washington State. This, in turn, may disqualify you for other assistance such as Medicaid, and it also means that you can't get at your money. In one outrageous example I was told about an advisor who locked one veteran's money into an annuity that wouldn't start paying out until he was well into his nineties!

• Also, some retirement homes are now using the lure of Aid and Attendance to get veterans to move in on the premise that they will get Aid and Attendance and it will pay for everything. In cases where the claim is denied after the veteran has already spent money to move in, this leaves the veteran in the untenable position of being unable to afford to remain in the facility.

We have also seen a flood of advertising in the past year urging those with VA home loans to refinance their homes. Veterans on my staff and elsewhere at the bureau have received a torrent of these offers in the mail. We were concerned enough that the Bureau and the FTC did a joint sweep of the mortgage ads which resulted in letters to a number of lenders concerning potential violations of the Mortgage Acts and Practices—Advertising (MAP) Rule, with the potential for future enforcement actions by the Bureau and FTC.

On a related note, I commend the FTC for its first enforcement action under the MAP Rule, announced June 27th, in which Mortgage Investors Corporation, a large refinancer of veterans' home loans, must pay a $7.5 million penalty for allegedly calling consumers on the Federal Trade Commission's National Do Not Call list, failing to remove consumers from its company call list upon demand, and misstating the terms of available loan products during telemarketing calls.

One last area of concern is pension advances—offers to pay military retirees a lump-sum payout in return for their monthly retirement payments. These offers usually amount to pennies on the dollar, and may be in violation of the law regarding assignment of pension benefits, even though they are disguised as loans. If you go on the internet you will find them—often with patriotic-sounding names and the

American flags on the Web site to match, but with a high cost for the retiree who takes them up on the offer.

The Bureau has an Office of Financial Protection for Older Americans and my office is working with them on these issues. They have recently reported to Congress on the wide array of ''elder financial advisor'' designations that are in use and spotlighted the fact that many of them are not based on any sort of academic rigor or significant training—but may sound official to elderly consumers.

To conclude, the Office of Servicemember Affairs is working hard to fulfill its mission to work on consumer financial education and consumer-protection measures for military personnel and their families, and we certainly want to include retirees and veterans in that number. We will press on to work with you and the States on existing problems and also address new issues as they arise. Our veterans and their families have done extraordinary service for our country, and, in return, it's an honor for me and my staff to serve them through our work at the Office of Servicemember Affairs.

Thank you for the opportunity to testify before the Committee.

———

RESPONSE TO POSTHEARING QUESTIONS SUBMITTED BY HON. JOHN D. ROCKEFELLER IV
TO CONSUMER FINANCIAL PROTECTION BUREAU

Question 1. Clearly, we are still recovering from the foreclosure crisis and the wrongdoing by the banks and mortgage servicers who repeatedly violated the SCRA. I know that unfortunately, some servicemembers are still fighting in court with their banks over these issues. What major issues are you seeing today in terms of violations of the SCRA?

Response. Senator, I was pleased to take part in the roundtable you held on the Servicemembers Civil Relief Act (SCRA) noncompliance issues that were so widespread in the mortgage market. As I noted in my testimony, while progress has been made and significant enforcement actions have been brought by the Department of Justice and the state Attorneys General, we do continue to see compliance concerns in the complaints that military/veteran consumers submit to the Bureau.

The SCRA issues I see are not limited to mortgage servicing; the Bureau has now identified other markets with similar problems. Most notably, in the student-loan servicing market, we've heard of lenders giving out incorrect or misleading information or even refusing to grant SCRA protections. Last October, my office, in conjunction with the Bureau's Office for Students, published a report documenting the SCRA concerns we had observed in student loan servicing. And, more recently, our Student Loan Ombudsman published a report in which he noted: ''While some lenders and servicers have addressed servicing problems facing military families since the publication of our previous report, not all have done so. The Bureau continues to receive complaints from servicemembers having trouble accessing benefits under the Servicemembers Civil Relief Act.''

———

RESPONSE TO POSTHEARING QUESTIONS SUBMITTED BY HON. MARK BEGICH TO
CONSUMER FINANCIAL PROTECTION BUREAU

Question 2. It's our understanding that that DOD and the CFPB have been collaborating together on a new financial readiness program to include SCRA education. What is the progress of that program, and in the meantime, what steps are being taken to educate servicemembers about their SCRA protections?

Response. In 2011, I personally observed the financial education given by Department of Defense to servicemembers at the beginning of their career: at Basic Training and the Advanced School that follows it. I watched financial classes at Naval Station Great Lakes (IL), the Army's Fort Jackson (SC) and the Marine Corps Recruit Depot in San Diego (CA).

My conclusion was that Basic Training is not a good place to absorb financial content, because recruits are tired and stressed, and even prone to fall asleep during the classes. Also, recruits may already be in debt before they arrive at Basic Training. Staff at Lackland Air Force Base, which conducts Air Force Basic Training, found that recruits arriving there in 2008 already had an average of $10,000 in debt.

Those two observations, among others, led the Bureau to plan to provide a short financial-education curriculum that can be accessed via smartphone or computer during what the military calls the Delayed Entry Program (DEP). DEP comprises the period when an individual has committed to join the military, but has not yet arrived at boot camp, and DEP can range from two weeks to up to a year in length.

It's a timeframe when a new recruit would have more time and less stress than at Basic Training so could focus on some "just-enough and just-in-time" financial lessons that could be very helpful before they get that first military paycheck and start thinking of ways to spend it. It could also provide useful information about Servicemember Civil Relief Act (SCRA) benefits for pre-service debt.

The Bureau is in the process of designing the modules and technical specifications to deliver this curriculum. We have sought and received input from the Pentagon, including the Senior Enlisted members of all the services, throughout the design process, and they have signaled their support for fielding the product when it is ready for an initial rollout.

My office has taken several other steps to help educate about the protections of the SCRA. For example, in March 2013 we hosted a virtual Military Financial Educator Forum on military student loan repayment issues, providing helpful information to military Personal Financial Managers, Education Service Officers, and Legal Assistance Attorneys. The interactive virtual forum highlighted military student loan servicing challenges and loan repayment options available to servicemembers, including the SCRA. Forum attendees were also provided with resource guides they could use to help their clients with this complex issue. Over 250 registered military educators and counselors logged in to view the forum from military installations all over the world including bases in the US, Japan, Germany, Belgium, Turkey, Djibouti and from ships off the coast of West Africa.

————

RESPONSE TO POSTHEARING QUESTIONS SUBMITTED BY HON. RICHARD BLUMENTHAL TO CONSUMER FINANCIAL PROTECTION BUREAU

Question 3. Failure to Include Open-end Credit Products in the DOD Definition of Consumer Credit

In 2007, following the passage of the Military Lending Act, the Department of Defense issued a regulation that exempted all forms of open-end credit products from the protections of the MLA. Even after acknowledging that open-end credit products such as military installment loans often have extremely high costs due to excessive fees and interest, the Department drafted a very narrow definition of consumer credit products.

Since 2007, many lenders have evolved and developed new practices by taking advantage of the Department's narrow definition. A report released last year by the Consumer Federation of America found evidence of this movement, concluding that "The trend in internet payday lending is toward longer-term 'installment' payment terms which places these triple-digit rate loans outside the 91-day term definition in the DOD rules." Another very popular form of high-cost loan used by servicemembers is a Deposit Advance product, which is a form of payday loan offered by a bank to an existing customer. Despite the fact that these type of open-end credit products are some of the most widely used among veterans, they are currently excluded from regulation under the Military Lending Act.

Ms. Petraeus, can you elaborate on how prevalent these open-end credit products are among military borrowers? If we do not close the loopholes in current regulation, do you expect lenders will continue offering closed-end credit products to servicemembers?

Response. I hear from financial counselors and Judge Advocate Generals (JAG) on the installations about the prevalence of payday-like products that are specifically marketed to military families—often with patriotic-sounding names and American flags on the Web site to match, but with a sky-high interest rate for the servicemember who takes out the loan. Although the Military Lending Act of 2007 ("Military Lending Act" or "MLA") put a 36 percent cap on the permissible interest rate of certain types of loans to the active-duty military, some lenders have found ways to get outside of the definitions in the Department of Defense (DOD) rule implementing the Military Lending Act.

For example, I know of one military-specific lender that offers loans with an annual percentage rate (APR) of over 500 percent, but structures its product as open-end credit so is not covered by the MLA. And unfortunately they aren't the only one. The internet is full of "military loans," some outright scams and others with very high interest rates.

While at Travis Air Force Base, CA, I also heard from a Personal Financial Manager whose airmen clients had taken out deposit advance products with triple-digit interest rates. The counselor and the base JAG were dismayed to find out that the MLA consumer protections did not apply because these products were structured as open-end credit.

However, structuring a product as open-end credit is not the only way to evade the protections of the MLA. A lender can also make their product longer than 91 days, make it greater than $2000, or even simply not require the borrower to provide a paycheck or Automated Clearing House (ACH) authorization as a payment mechanism. I have seen examples of all of these types of products marketed directly to servicemembers and their families. So yes, I am worried that we are seeing a shift away from products that are covered by the MLA to non-covered products and I fear that unless the regulations are updated the MLA will no longer provide the necessary consumer protections for military families.

Question 4. The Current Definition Undermines the Private Right of Action

The Military Lending Act of 2007 was a landmark piece of legislation that provided much needed financial protections for the men and women who serve our country. However, these protections are only effective if servicemembers have the ability to hold predatory lenders accountable when they break the law. Last year, I introduced legislation to establish a private right of action for veterans who have fallen victim to abusive lending practices. I was proud to see this legislation adopted and passed as an amendment to the National Defense Authorization Act of 2013.

However, even with the addition of this enforcement mechanism, the Military Lending Act is only effective if it is implemented through strong regulation. Unfortunately, the current Department of Defense regulations include a very narrow definition of consumer credit that exempts open-end credit products. The loophole created by this narrow definition allows lenders to offer high-cost, open-end credit products with annual percentage rates of 300 percent or more.

Though servicemembers are able to take action against lenders who have offered them credit products covered by current regulation, lenders are offering open-end credit products that are exempt from regulation with increasing frequency. We must revisit and strengthen these regulations to ensure that servicemembers and veterans are protected against the credit products that they use most.

Ms. Petraeus, can you talk about how the current exemption for open-end credit products undermines the ability of servicemembers to hold predatory lenders accountable?

Response. When the Military Lending Act of 2007 ("Military Lending Act" or "MLA") protections are applied only to a narrow band of credit products, there is less opportunity for regulators and enforcement agencies to protect military consumers from high-cost, high-risk loans. As you know well, an enforcement or private right of action can only take place if the credit product falls within the definition of consumer credit as defined by the Department of Defense in the MLA regulations. For example, even if a servicemember or their spouse takes out a payday loan with an APR in excess of 36 percent, agencies with administrative enforcement authority under the law are unable to enforce the protections of the MLA if that loan is greater than 91 days, over $2000, or structured as open-end credit. So it is very important that the Department of Defense is reexamining the regulation and the current definition of "consumer credit."

RESPONSE TO POSTHEARING QUESTIONS SUBMITTED BY HON. MAZIE HIRONO TO CONSUMER FINANCIAL PROTECTION BUREAU

Question 5. Your testimony describes the practices of some colleges who aggressively recruit servicemembers just for their GI Bill benefits. Veterans can be targeted to sign up, even if they aren't qualified for the courses. As one possible cause, your testimony points to a loophole in the "90–10" rule, in which GI Bill benefits aren't considered education benefits subject to the 90% limit on some colleges' Federal funds. Do you support legislation to close this loophole and put GI Bill Benefits on the same footing as U.S. Department of Education (ED) benefits in the 90–10 rule?

Response. The overall cost to the government of the GI Bill and Tuition Assistance (TA) has soared since passage of the 90–10 rule. According to Department of Veterans Affairs (VA) records, while the number of individuals using VA education benefits has roughly doubled since 1998—from less than 500,000 recipients to nearly 1 million—the monetary cost has grown ten-fold, rising from less than one billion to nearly ten and a half billion dollars per year. And the cost of TA has also grown exponentially, on what I have heard described as an unsustainable upward trajectory, with for-profit colleges taking an increasing share of those TA dollars. In 2011, for-profit colleges collected one of every two TA dollars, totaling $280 million of the $563 million disbursed during the year. This is an 8 percent increase over 2009, when for-profit schools collected 42 percent of the $515 million in TA funds disbursed. It seems prudent for policymakers to examine whether the 90–10 rule in its current form is a sensible framework, given the significant increase in the number of servicemembers, veterans, and military spouses receiving education benefits.

Question 6. What other specific legislation should Congress pass to better protect taxpayers, veterans, and their families in the use of Federal GI Bill benefits?

Response. As an independent regulatory agency, the Bureau is focused on carrying out, implementing, and enforcing the laws that Congress and the President enact. We would be happy to meet with you or your staff to discuss Federal GI Bill benefits and our concerns with protecting taxpayers, veterans, and their families.

The Bureau has been working in concert with the VA, Department of Defense, Department of Education, and the Department of Justice to implement Executive Order 13607, "Establishing Principles of Excellence for Educational Institutions Serving Servicemembers, Veterans, Spouses, and Other Family Members" and the Comprehensive Veterans Education Information Policy law (PL 112–249).

Chairman SANDERS. You finished on military precision with 5 seconds to go. Thank you.

Colonel Kantwill.

STATEMENT OF COLONEL PAUL KANTWILL, DIRECTOR OF LEGAL POLICY, OFFICE OF THE UNDERSECRETARY FOR PERSONNEL AND READINESS, U.S. DEPARTMENT OF DEFENSE

Colonel KANTWILL. Good morning, Mr. Chairman, Senator Boozman, and Members of the Committee. It is an honor to appear before you and represent the Department of Defense and all of our great men and women. On behalf of the Department, I thank you for your assistance and support in protecting our servicemembers and their families in the consumer financial marketplace, and for the opportunity to address you today regarding financial issues affecting them.

I will discuss first the SCRA. I will then discuss other financial challenges confronting servicemembers and their families in today's marketplace, focusing on issues and challenges that fall within or around the Military Lending Act, or MLA, as the Department sees this as the biggest current financial challenge facing our force.

The Department recognizes and appreciates fully the critical importance of the SCRA. No other statute provides the breadth of benefits and protections for servicemembers that the SCRA does, and over its long history of more than 70 years it has lessened some of the very many burdens associated with military service.

Congress has continued to play the most critical role in protecting our servicemembers and their families, strengthening the Act and its protections in many ways, especially in recent years. It is with pride, therefore, that we assert that the current status of the SCRA education compliance and enforcement is largely a good news story. We have all read accounts of mortgage foreclosure abuses and we know well the ravages that the economic crisis and the burdens of more than 12 years of deployments have had upon the financial fitness of military families.

As these relate to the SCRA, however, we believe we have been very effective in curbing foreclosure abuses against military personnel and their families. This is the result of much sustained and very hard work within the Department and with other Governmental agencies and the financial industry.

The Department is fortunate to enjoy a tremendous relationship with other Federal agencies relating to consumer law issues, the Department of Justice and CFPB and the OCC, to name just a few.

Federal enforcement actions brought by our colleagues at Justice have been swift and effective. We are pleased to have the CFPB always at our side. State and local compliance and enforcement efforts are critical.

There may still be foreclosures out there. We may not be yet out of the economic woods, and we are looking closely at some issues like the reduction of interest rates on student loans under the SCRA, but we are largely encouraged by good progress on the SCRA front.

Despite the successes that we can cite on the SCRA, we have concerns regarding small dollar lending and related products and services. Since significant departmental, interagency, and Congressional action resulted in the Military Lending Act more than 7 years ago, we have stamped out the majority of abuses in the areas regulated.

Several years removed from its enactment, however, many parties from servicemembers to State Attorneys Generals express concerns that the industry, including some unscrupulous lenders, have sought and are seeking to create products and services which fall outside the MLA.

This has not escaped our or Congress's attention that at your direction the Department is studying changes in the credit marketplace and their effects on servicemembers and their families. The Department's advance notice of proposed rulemaking was published in June 2013.

While many groups apprise us that our concerns are well-advised, the Department is undertaking its own extensive surveys to gather even more information. A survey of DOD legal assistance personnel around the world closes out tomorrow. A similar survey has been distributed to DOD financial counselors. Last, a larger survey is being sent to our servicemembers, the boots on the ground, if you will.

The Department has assembled the Prudential Regulators and the CFPB to explore potential revisions to the regulation. We have assembled a team of skilled economists, analysts, and drafters to assist us in this initial rulemaking. We will analyze our responses to the Federal Register notice in order to obtain a broad basis of feedback from consumer advocates, the financial industries, Federal and State regulators, and engaged citizens in order to determine the potential benefits, pitfalls, and consequences of extending the definitions of the regulation to cover additional forms of credit.

We remain committed to balancing regulation with education and assistance to maintain financial readiness, and the Department plans to maintain a steady approach to implementing the regulation to balance the protections offered through the regulation, while sustaining access to helpful, financial products.

In response to these challenges and in support of our servicemembers and their families, the Department remains proactive and vigilant, employing multifaceted education and training programs and leveraging all available resources. On behalf of the Department, I thank you for your assistance and support. It is my privilege to appear before you and I look forward to your questions.

[The prepared statement of Colonel Kantwill follows:]

PREPARED STATEMENT OF COLONEL PAUL KANTWILL, DIRECTOR, OFFICE OF LEGAL POLICY, OFFICE OF THE UNDER SECRETARY OF DEFENSE (PERSONNEL & READINESS), U.S. DEPARTMENT OF DEFENSE

Good Morning, Chairman Sanders, Ranking Member Burr, and Members of the Committee. It is an honor to appear before you and represent the Department of Defense and all of our great men and women in uniform. On behalf of the Department, I thank you for your assistance and support in protecting our Servicemembers and their families in the consumer financial marketplace. It is a pleasure to testify before you regarding the consumer financial issues we see affecting Servicemembers, Veterans, and their families and the Department's response to these issues and challenges.

I should first like to provide a bit of background on the current state of the Department's involvement in consumer law issues and financial readiness. I will then turn my focus to the Servicemember's Civil Relief Act (SCRA), with specific focus on the Department's efforts to support compliance and enforcement thereof. Third, I will discuss other financial challenges confronting Servicemembers, veterans, and their families in today's consumer marketplace. These challenges are many and varied, but I will focus primarily on issues and challenges that fall within or around the Military Lending Act (MLA)—small dollar, payday-type lending services and products—as the Department sees this as the biggest, current financial challenge facing our Servicemembers, Veterans, and their families. I will conclude with some very specific observations on where the Department sees the consumer credit industry going and the actions currently underway in very specific response to these developments.

DEPARTMENT OF DEFENSE FINANCIAL READINESS PROGRAMS

The financial readiness of Servicemembers and their families is essential to their well-being and their ability to contribute to the mission. Over the course of my career as a Judge Advocate, I have assisted Servicemembers and their families in deployed and garrison environments, and know well that a Servicemember distracted from the tactical mission by financial issues cannot be completely mission-focused. Thus, the Department has, for over a decade, created, refined, and enhanced financial readiness programs predicated on Servicemembers and their families receiving reasonable protections, acquiring at least a basic understanding of finances, and receiving access to helpful financial products and services.

Since the term "Financial Readiness" was first coined in 2003, the Department has continually improved and expanded its financial readiness campaign to increase Servicemember awareness of saving and financial stability, and enhance understanding of financial products and services. Utilizing a combination of education, resources, programs, and protections (such as the SCRA and the MLA), the campaign's goal is to reduce the financial stress on military families, thereby enhancing overall mission readiness.

The Financial Readiness Campaign involves eight pillars of financial readiness:
1. Maintaining good credit
2. Achieving financial stability
3. Establishing routine savings
4. Participation in the Thrift Savings Plan and Savings Deposit Program
5. Retention of the Servicemember's Group Life Insurance and other insurance
6. Utilization of low-cost loan products as an alternative to payday lending and predatory loans
7. Use of low-cost Morale, Welfare and Recreation programs such as the Commissary and PX
8. Preservation of Security Clearances

The campaign has been effective and is on-going. Servicemember participation in the Thrift Savings Program, for example, is at an all-time high. The Savings Deposit Program, available to all deployed Servicemembers, enjoys similarly historic high participation rates. The campaign is augmented by nonprofit organizations that produce programs and campaigns such as "SaveandInvest.org" and "Military Saves." The recent "Military Saves" campaign was the largest and best ever.

An essential element of our Personal Financial Readiness Program is proactive life cycle financial management services. The program addresses the effects of financial decisions on personal and professional lives, provides resources needed to make prudent consumer decisions, and offers related services and support.

A variety of resources are available to help Servicemembers and their families avoid the consequences of poor financial decisions, and to put them on the path to financial freedom. Education, counseling, and training are available both on-line and in-person to military members and families of all components. The Department has Personal Finance Managers (PFMs) at every military installation who provide financial counseling, education, training, and services. All of these PFMs hold a nationally recognized financial counselor certification.

As part of the DOD Military Family Life Consultants (MFLC) program, the Department has additional resources in the form of Personal Financial Counselors (PFCs) who augment other resources and provide "surge" capability to units or installations at critical times or with critical needs.

Other excellent resources, such as Military OneSource (MOS) are available 24 hours per day for all Servicemembers and their families. MOS offers free and confidential financial consultations over the phone or face-to-face, in addition to providing specialized financial and tax planning consultations. The "Money" section of MilitaryOneSource.com provides financial information and resources that include calculators, tips, books and CDs, and personal finance newsletters.

The Department has also partnered with nationally-recognized, financial literacy non-profit organizations. Groups like the Consumer Federation of America (CFA), the Better Business Bureau Military Line, and the Financial Industry Regulatory Authority (FINRA) Education Foundation provide tremendous resources free of charge. The Department and CFA conduct the tremendously-successful Military Saves Campaign every year. DOD also partners with the Department of the Treasury and the Federal Trade Commission (FTC)—just two of more than twenty such organizations with whom we work in Treasury's Financial Literacy and Education Commission) to address consumer awareness, identity theft, and insurance scams to Servicemembers and families.

THE SERVICEMEMBER'S CIVIL RELIEF ACT

The Department recognizes and appreciates the critical importance of the SCRA. It is clear that no other statute provides such a unique breadth of benefits and protections for Servicemembers. The purpose of the SCRA is a lofty one, to provide Servicemembers' peace of mind, knowing that their personal affairs and economic interests will be protected while they put their lives on the line in defense of our Nation, and the Act has lived up to that goal.

The Act's protections are broad and diverse. It protects Servicemembers from evictions, default judgments, and foreclosure. It allows them to delay judicial proceedings and to place caps on their interest rates. It also provides them and their spouses certain tax relief. Over its long history of more than 70 years, it has lessened some of the many burdens associated with military service.

CONGRESSIONAL EFFORTS TO STRENGTHEN ENFORCEMENT OF THE SCRA

Congress has continued to play a most critical role in protecting our Servicemembers and their families. Over the last few years Congress has strengthened the SCRA's protections through such measures as the Veterans' Benefit Act of 2010, which provided for additional civil enforcement, as well as monetary damages and attorneys' fees. It also clarified that the Attorney General has similar enforcement authority on behalf of Servicemembers and other aggrieved persons.

Congress has extended the 6% interest rate cap for pre-service mortgage obligations. This interest rate cap, which had been in effect for decades, had previously applied only to actual periods of active duty. Now the interest rate cap for pre-service mortgage obligations has been extended for an additional 12 months after leaving active duty. Congress also amended the SCRA to extend protections from foreclosure on pre-service mortgage obligations for twelve months after the Servicemember leaves active duty. Under these conditions and during this time, no Servicemember cannot be foreclosed upon absent a court order.

SCRA Education and Enforcement

Congressional support through the SCRA and other measures, however, means little if our Servicemembers are not aware of their rights. Thus, the Department has developed programs to ensure that Servicemembers know about the benefits and protections of the SCRA. This educational process involves coordinated and overlapping efforts to alert the Servicemembers and their commanders of these benefits and protections and then to ensure that the proper counselors are there to help the Servicemember fully understand the nuances of the relevant laws and receive their full protections under the law.

The Department's efforts to educate servicemembers and their families center around installation readiness facilities, pre-deployment and re-deployment process facilities, and reserve component mobilization and demobilization processing centers. These reserve component processing centers have been of critical importance because two of the most important economic protections and benefits—the 6% interest rate cap and the extension of foreclosure protections—apply only to pre-service obligations and thus effect predominately Reservists and National Guardsmen called to active duty. As a result, SCRA and related financial training at pre-deployment and re-deployment processing facilities is more detailed and helpful than ever before.

Thus, it is with pride we assert that SCRA education, compliance, and enforcement is a "good news story." Certainly there have been accounts of mortgage foreclosure abuses and other prominent SCRA violations. We know well, the ravages the economic crisis and burdens of more than 12 years of sustained conflict with related deployments have had upon the financial fitness of military families.

As it relates particularly to the SCRA, however, we have been effective in curbing foreclosure abuses against military personnel and their families. While there may still be some foreclosures in process or in the "pipeline," it appears that the majority of the abuses seen in the past have been curbed. This is the result of sustained and hard work within the Department, with other government agencies, as well as with the financial industry.

The Department is fortunate to enjoy—as you can see from our collective presence here today—a very cooperative working relationship with other Federal agencies relating to consumer law issues—the Department of Justice, the CFPB, the CFPB's Office of Servicemember's Affairs (OSA), and the Office of the Comptroller of the Currency (OCC), to name just a few. Federal enforcement actions brought by our colleagues at Justice have been swift and effective. State and local compliance and enforcement efforts are critical. We are grateful for our cooperative working relationships with consumer advocates and other organizations such as the Consumer Federation of America (CFA) and the HOPE NOW Alliance, dedicated to assisting all persons with their financial needs—but who are also tremendously dedicated to our military families.

We have been and remain engaged with the consumer financial industry. If we are to represent and protect our Servicemembers and their families—and we will— it is essential to have open lines of communication with the industry. We are proud of our cooperation with the American Bankers Association, the Association of Military Bankers of America, the Credit Union National Association, and the Defense Credit Union Council, in efforts to keep them apprised on the SCRA and the MLA, and advise them of issues affecting our Force. Our close working relationship with the Financial Services Roundtable (FSR) and the Housing Policy Council (HPC) has allowed us to advocate frequently and effectively on financial issues affecting the Force. The industry remains supportive and complementary of the Department's enhancements to the Defense Manpower Data Center's database capabilities, providing industry with real-time, public-access, large batch data search capabilities and allowing industry to identify military customers and provide them SCRA and other benefits to which they are entitled. Other initiatives include forms, accepted by the financial industry, that allow Servicemembers to invoke their SCRA protections more easily. Our work with industry and other agencies has already produced great developments regarding protections and benefits for military families disadvantaged by Permanent Change of Station (PCS) moves.

In conclusion, while there may be more foreclosures on the horizon, and we are not yet out of the "economic woods," we are very encouraged by solid progress on the SCRA front.

THE MILITARY LENDING ACT AND RELATED FINANCIAL CHALLENGES

Despite the aforementioned successes on the SCRA front, we have commensurate concerns regarding small dollar lending and related products and services. Seven years ago, the Department recognized there were some specific lending practices causing problems for Servicemembers and their families, which could not be adequately addressed through education programs and awareness campaigns. Significant Departmental and Inter-Agency action resulted in our Report on Predatory Lending Practices Directed at Members of the Armed Forces and Their Dependents (2006), and subsequent Congressional action in the form of the Talent Amendment, commonly referred to as the Military Lending Act (MLA) (Sec 670 of the John Warner National Defense Authorization Act for FY 2007). The MLA gave the Department authority to write a regulation to define "credit" subject to the limitations posed by the MLA.

With the assistance of the Prudential Regulatory Agencies we did just that, and the resulting rule (32 CFR Part 232) covered and tax refund anticipation loans and closed-end payday loans and vehicle title loans—both of which are tightly defined,. This good work stamped out the majority of abuses in the areas regulated, and we have relied upon the enforcement efforts of Federal and state regulators to great effect.

The Department has remained vigilant in this area. Annually, we send a representative to the National Conference of Consumer Credit Administrators to ensure uniformity in compliance by covered creditors. Each year the regulators have reported that their examinations have found compliance with the Rule and no need for enforcement action. In some states where such loans are authorized, but in which enforcement authority has not been provided to, the Department has engaged the States, requesting they make technical amendments to their statutes allowing for administrative enforcement. To date, 37 States either do not authorize these loans or provide their regulators with adequate administrative enforcement authority.

The Department has also been working with the FTC and the CFPB to assist in recording violations of the SCRA and the MLA in the FTC's law enforcement database—Military Sentinel. DOD legal assistance attorneys and financial counselors assist military clients with recording instances of fraud, deception, abusive practices, and identity theft into the database so U.S. Attorneys, State Attorneys General, Federal and state regulators, and other law enforcement agencies have access to allegations.

Our Servicemembers, families, Veterans, legal assistance attorneys, and financial counselors have informed us that the MLA legislation has been extremely effective in stamping out abuses involving the types of credit covered. In addition, Relief Societies, military banks, and credit unions have assisted Servicemembers and families in need. Despite this success, unscrupulous lenders have sought, and are seeking, to create products and services which fall outside of the MLA and the enforcement actions mentioned above.

Several years removed from its enactment, however, our financial counselors and legal assistance attorneys still see clients who have payday or vehicle title loans. They also report that internet and overseas opportunities exist to evade the law, and that some unscrupulous lenders—and even borrowers—still attempt to skirt or evade the law, by entering into loans that charge interest greater than 36 percent and contain terms that have been modified to avoid falling under the MLA. Creditors and lenders still attempt to avoid the MLA by utilizing procedures or modifying products to fall outside of the regulation.

Lending over the internet remains an issue, with the most egregious offenders located off-shore or outside the U.S. to avoid coverage under the Act. The use of allotments in consumer credit transactions and the abuse of installments loans are of concern to the Department.

THE DEPARTMENT'S EFFORTS

This has not escaped our—or Congress'—attention, and at the direction of the Congress, the Department is studying changes in the credit marketplace and their effects on Servicemembers and their families. The first notice of this study was posted in the *Federal Register* on June 13, 2013, and we expect to receive comments by August 1, 2013.

While our close cooperation with Governmental entities, non-profit organizations, and consumer watchdog groups—as well as our own efforts—have apprised us that our collective concerns are well-placed, the Department is undertaking its own extensive, internal surveys to gather even more information. A survey of DOD Legal Assistance Personnel has been sent to legal offices across the globe. The intent of the survey is to learn from practitioners, with hands-on experience assisting clients in consumer law matters, which financial products and issues are most prevalent in the force today, and we are currently receiving responses. A similar survey is being distributed to DOD financial counselors. Last, a larger-scale survey has been sent to servicemembers, the "boots-on-the-ground."

As a result of what we have learned thus far, the Department has assembled the Prudential Regulatory Agencies and the CFPB to explore revisions to the regulation. We have established a team of skilled economists and analysts to assist us in this initial rulemaking, in addition to a similarly-skilled team of drafters. From all of these sources, and with all of this assistance, we will determine the best course our proposed rulemaking should take.

As our investigation progresses, and in response to these challenges and in support of our Servicemembers and their families, the Department remains proactive and vigilant; employing multi-faceted education and training programs, and leveraging all available resources, including extensive cooperation with all of the Agencies and partners described above.

The Services Legal Assistance Programs have continued to provide expert legal assistance in all consumer law areas. These services, focused where needed at the installation level, are available to assist in a large number of Consumer Law related areas. These include services in all the areas noted above, to include the burgeoning areas of suspect auto loans/purchase practices, deployment-related SCRA violations, and aggressive debt collection practices.

The Services continue to designate Consumer Law matters in their highest tiers of available services and provide specialized training is provided to all practitioners. The Department's long-term association with the Legal Assistance for Military Practitioners (LAMP) Committee of the American Bar Association (ABA) and its Pro Bono Project (PBP), enables the Services' Legal Assistance organizations to refer eligible clients to the PBP, where they receive both in- and out-of court-representation from local volunteer attorneys who are subject matter experts in Consumer Law. The PBP has been so successful that the ABA has pushed the concept to state and local bar associations, who are now offering very similar programs in conjunction with their local military installations.

THE WAY AHEAD

Current efforts of the Department, other Government agencies, and non-profit organizations are important. But even more important are future efforts to protect and advocate for our Servicemembers, the way ahead on consumer law issues affecting the force, and how we work to meet those challenges.

The Department is reviewing all available evidence and data, and pending the results of the surveys described above, we will review options for appropriate action with our partners. We will carefully analyze responses to our *Federal Register* notice in order to obtain a broad basis of feedback from consumer advocates, the financial industry, Federal and state regulators, and engaged citizens in order to determine the potential benefits, pitfalls, and unintended consequences of extending the definitions in the regulation to cover additional forms of payday, vehicle title, and tax refund anticipation loans, as well as other forms of financial products not covered by the regulation currently. We remain committed to balancing regulation with education and assistance to maintain the financial readiness of the force. The MLA and implementing regulation have done what was intended over the past six years, and the Department plans to maintain a steady approach to the implementing regulation to balance the protections offered through the regulation while sustaining unimpeded access to helpful financial products.

On behalf of the Department, I thank you for your assistance and support. It is my privilege to appear before you and I look forward to your questions.

RESPONSE TO POSTHEARING QUESTIONS SUBMITTED BY HON. MARK BEGICH TO THE U.S. DEPARTMENT OF DEFENSE

Question 1. Can you outline for us progress made to date on improving DMDC and what future plans DOD has to improve the SCRA processing component of DMDC?

Response. DMDC has continuously improved the SCRA application and Web site since its inception, balancing the concerns of industry, Consumer Financial Protection Bureau requirements, and individual privacy interests. Below is the timeline of DMDC's efforts to respond to SCRA inquiries:

Prior to 2002—DMDC responded to inquiries on SCRA eligibility manually. The inquiries were received through the mail or over the telephone.

In 2002—DMDC developed and launched the SCRA Website. All users had to establish accounts. The Web site only provided responses on those members currently serving on active duty.

April 2005—DMDC converted SCRA Website to a public site.

August 2009—DMDC expanded the Web site to answer the question "has this individual served on active duty in the last 367 days." This was done to address changes in the law that extended protections beyond their actual dates of service.

January 2010—DMDC added CAPTCHA (Completely Automated Public Turing test to tell Computers and Humans Apart) to the site to prevent "screen scraping" This added an additional level of security to prevent computer-generated requests intended to capture large amounts of data for commercial re-sale. After many complaints, in April 2011 CAPTCHA was removed.

Late 2011—DMDC added the ability to query historic periods of active duty back to 1985. In addition, outside the Web site, DMDC provided extensive support to institutional customers being audited by the DoJ and Treasury.

April 2012—DMDC made several enhancements to the Web site. The manual process above was made available through the Multiple Record Request option. The match criteria for an individual were updated to include not only Social Security Number (SSN) and last name but also to match on last name and date of birth. This change was necessary because not all users have ready access to or can ask for SSN.

February 2013—SCRA 3.0 (the most current version) was released. This version was well received by the financial industry. DMDC consolidated the single and multiple requests into a single code base. It also tightened the rules for matching on last name from the first three characters only to the complete submitted last name. The final change was the addition of a news display that DMDC uses for informing users of any upcoming changes to the site or issues the site may be having.

As new technology becomes available, DMDC will continue to improve the SCRA Web site and ensure that changes do not compromise the privacy of the individual or the security of the DMDC infrastructure.

Question 2. To DOD and CFPB-It's our understanding that that DOD and the CFPB have been collaborating together on a new financial readiness program to include SCRA education. What is the progress of that program, and in the meantime, what steps are being taken to educate servicemembers about their SCRA protections?

Response. The Department has developed many and varied programs to ensure that Servicemembers know about the benefits and protections of the SCRA. This educational process involves coordinated and overlapping efforts to alert the Servicemembers and their commanders of these benefits and protections and then to ensure that the proper counselors are there to help the Servicemember fully understand the nuances of the relevant laws and receive their full protections under the law. The Department's efforts to educate servicemembers and their families center around installation readiness facilities, pre-deployment and re-deployment process facilities, and reserve component mobilization and demobilization processing centers. These reserve component processing centers have been of critical importance because two of the most important economic protections and benefits-the 6% interest rate cap and the extension of foreclosure protections-apply only to pre-service obligations and thus effect predominately Reservists and National Guardsmen called to active duty. As a result, SCRA and related financial training at pre-deployment and re-deployment processing facilities is more detailed and helpful than ever before.

The CFPB has played, and will play, an important role in education and enforcement. The CFPB's Office of Servicemember Affairs works with DOD to educate and empower Servicemembers and their families to make better (OSA) informed consumer decisions, to monitor military complaints to the Bureau and the responses to those complaints, and to coordinate with Federal and state agencies on consumer protection measures for the military. For example, the OSA worked with DOD to create the financial module for the DOD Transition Assistance Program, or TAP.

DOD and CFPB will continue to work together to ensure that regulations and policies that provide legal protections for consumers do not unintentionally hamper Servicemembers and military families from accessing those legal protections and to ensure Servicemembers have a thorough knowledge of current law. While there is no "silver bullet" product or one-size-fits all solution for the consumer financial needs of and protections for the military community, DOD and CFPB employ a multi-faceted approach consisting of career-spanning financial education and coaching; military-friendly financial products from financial-services providers; enhanced consumer financial tools and targeted regulatory protection guidelines; all of which can go a long way toward addressing and mitigating the consumer financial challenges of the military community.

RESPONSE TO POSTHEARING QUESTIONS SUBMITTED BY HON. RICHARD BLUMENTHAL TO THE U.S. DEPARTMENT OF DEFENSE

Question 3. Failure to Include Open-end Credit Products in the DOD Definition of Consumer Credit

In 2007, following the passage of the Military Lending Act, the Department of Defense issued a regulation that exempted all forms of open-end credit products from the protections of the MLA. Even after acknowledging that open-end credit products such as military installment loans often have extremely high costs due to excessive fees and interest, the Department drafted a very narrow definition of consumer credit products.

Since 2007, many lenders have evolved and developed new practices by taking advantage of the Department's narrow definition. A report released last year by the Consumer Federation of America found evidence of this movement, concluding that

''The trend in internet payday lending is toward longer-term 'installment' payment terms which places these triple-digit rate loans outside the 91-day term definition in the DOD rules.'' Another very popular form of high-cost loan used by servicemembers is a Deposit Advance product, which is a form of payday loan offered by a bank to an existing customer. Despite the fact that these type of open-end credit products are some of the most widely used among veterans, they are currently excluded from regulation under the Military Lending Act.

Colonel Kantwill, will the Department's review of its Military Lending Act regulations include an effort to make sure that veterans are protected from high costs on the open-end credit products they use most frequently, such as installment loans and Deposit Advance products?

Response. The Department of Defense recognizes that the regulation is overdue for revision. We requested the assistance of the Prudential Regulators and the Consumer Financial Protection Bureau in February of this year to prepare for the review requested in the Conference Report accompanying the National Defense Authorization Act for Fiscal Year 2013. As a result of their consultation, we are conducting preliminary rulemaking while accomplishing the review intended by the Report. We requested public input that would assist informing our report, and used it also as a way of letting the public know of our intent to propose a revision to the existing regulation. We received 34 responses to our Advanced Notice of Proposed Rulemaking. These responses recognize the importance of the Military Lending Act and its successful impact on curbing the availability of high cost-short term loans. The majority of the responses also recommend that DOD expand the definitions in the rule. We anticipate using these inputs to assist in developing a proposed rule by the end of the calendar year.

Question 4. The Current Definition Undermines the Private Right of Action

The Military Lending Act of 2007 was a landmark piece of legislation that provided much needed financial protections for the men and women who serve our country. However, these protections are only effective if servicemembers have the ability to hold predatory lenders accountable when they break the law. Last year, I introduced legislation to establish a private right of action for veterans who have fallen victim to abusive lending practices. I was proud to see this legislation adopted and passed as an amendment to the National Defense Authorization Act of 2013.

However, even with the addition of this enforcement mechanism, the Military Lending Act is only effective if it is implemented through strong regulation. Unfortunately, the current Department of Defense regulations include a very narrow definition of consumer credit that exempts open-end credit products. The loophole created by this narrow definition allows lenders to offer high-cost, open-end credit products with annual percentage rates of 300 percent or more.

Though servicemembers are able to take action against lenders who have offered them credit products covered by current regulation, lenders are offering open-end credit products that are exempt from regulation with increasing frequency. We must revisit and strengthen these regulations to ensure that servicemembers and veterans are protected against the credit products that they use most.

Colonel Kantwill, does the Department make any effort to educate servicemembers of their right to take action against predatory lenders? How frequently have veterans used the private right of action since its establishment? Do you think that the Department can take steps to ensure that the private right of action is used more frequently?

Response. The establishing a Servicemember's private right of action provides a meaningful enforcement capability that can hold creditors accountable to the borrower for their credit practices. We believe that the private right of action, along with added enforcement by the Consumer Financial Protection Bureau (CFPB), enhances current enforcement by state regulators to assure covered creditors will comply. We also understand that the current definitions of credit in the regulation are no longer adequate to cover the products that are potentially causing concern, so the Department is working with the Prudential Regulators and the CFPB to revise the regulation.

The Department is also fully engaged in educating Servicemembers concerning their rights as consumers, so that they are familiar with their rights under Federal consumer law, Servicemembers Civil Relief Act (SCRA), and the Military Lending Act (MLA). Indeed, as I indicated in my oral and written testimony, The Department's efforts to educate servicemembers and their families center around installation readiness facilities, pre-deployment and re-deployment process facilities, and reserve component mobilization and demobilization processing centers. This education and training is more sophisticated and detailed that it has even been. A validation of the Department's efforts is the fact that several of the largest SCRA-related enforcement actions originated with SMs and their legal assistance attorneys working together to enforce those very important rights. In addition, we are aware of additional litigation launched by private attorneys on behalf of Servicemembers as a class. Thus, we are aware of significant litigation involving SCRA protections and at least one on-going case in Georgia concerning the MLA. We hope that continued education about the MLA will preclude Servicemembers and their family members making use of prohibited credit products, essentially reducing the potential for litigation. In the event that a military borrower obtains a covered loan (without deceiving the creditor or colluding with the creditor), legal assistance attorneys and financial counselors will advise borrowers of their rights to take private action. Whether they wish to do so will still be their option.

————

RESPONSE TO POSTHEARING QUESTIONS SUBMITTED BY HON. MAZIE HIRONO TO
THE U.S. DEPARTMENT OF DEFENSE

Question 5. In your testimony you mention that the Department "has Personal Finance Managers (PFMs) at every installation." Does this mean that Ft. Bragg has a single PFM to service around 60,000 troops? What is the distribution of PFMs at Army installations in Hawaii?

Response. Fort Bragg's Financial Readiness Program (FRP) has 19 dedicated FPMs currently assigned to improve soldiers' personal financial status and their abilities to act as informed consumers. Direct assistance is provided to unit commanders and leaders on training Soldiers and family members in personal financial readiness. The Fort Bragg FRP also works closely with the adjacent Pope Air Force Base Airman and Family Readiness Center to ensure that Servicemembers and their families have access to one-on-one counseling services, as well as broad range of classes, workshops, and community resources to help military families meet their financial goals.

Similarly, our PFMs have a robust presence of financial experts at Army installations in Hawaii. For example, the Army Community Service FRP at Schofield Barracks, Hawaii team has a versatile, professional team ready to serve Soldiers and family members, which includes over 10 service providers, including four personal financial counselors and financial readiness specialists, a Military Family Life Consultant, an Army Emergency Relief officer, a social service representative, and two financial literacy instructors. The FRP stands ready and willing to assist all Soldiers, even those currently downrange. Additionally, the Military Family and Support Center (MFSC) is a newly established joint service center which synergizes the resources and know-how of Pearl Harbor's Fleet & Family Support Center and Hickam's Airman & Family Readiness Center.

Across the Services, our knowledgeable, well-trained and experienced teams of social workers, educators and specialists provide assistance and community-based support to military families on everything from employment aid, education and counseling on money matters, and affordance access to childcare. Additionally, the "Military Saves" campaign, co-sponsored by the Consumer Federation of America and the Department of Defense, has now become an integral part of the Department of Defense's comprehensive Financial Readiness Campaign. This past year alone, Military Saves reached 137,392 servicemembers and families directly by installation efforts, along with another 163,000 through Facebook, 1.6 million Twitter impressions, and 35,000 visits to MilitarySaves.org. As led by "our boots on the ground" PFMs, the Department continues to develop a military command climate and overall culture that supports prudent financial behavior through financial literacy education and counseling.

Question 6. Your testimony states that "at critical times or with critical needs." there are additional resources—i.e. more PFMs, which you refer to as "surge" capability. Are these called upon in lecture setting only to meet with pre-deploying or re-deploying soldiers, or are they also used for servicemembers who are undergoing a permanent change of station or approaching their expiration term of service?

Response. Through our Family Readiness System, the Department provides a broad range of financial management services to give our Active duty, Guard/Reserve and their families, regardless of mobilization status, the tools they need to achieve personal financial goals and address financial challenges at all at stages of a military career. Personal Financial Managers (PFMs) at military installations provide financial counseling and consultation services, ranging from budgeting, saving, debt reduction, consumer advocacy and complaint resolution, referral for emergency funds, financial workshops, retirement planning, and education programs for youth and teens. This includes proactive educational classes and workshops for the entire military community, as well as focused "one-on-one" professional financial counseling. In 2013, our PFMs provided over 34,867 briefings to a total of 872,187 participants, and provided individual counseling to 1,828,299 individuals, including 161,992 in-depth extended contacts.

Moreover, as part of the Military Family Life Consultants (MFLC) program, our Personal Financial Counselors (PFCs) are available for "surge" support assignments for bases and other units. PFCs augment the support offered by the Military Services PFMs to troops and families by providing financial education classes and workshops, counseling, and other assistance, especially in conjunction with planned deployment cycle events. Our financial readiness programs are focused on a 24/7 lifecycle delivery system that starts with mandatory entry-level training and progresses throughout a Servicemember's military career, to transition retiring and separating members successfully back into civilian life.

Through this collaborative and comprehensive approach, our PFMs and PFCs support commanders in keeping Servicemembers and family members financially prepared and aware, such as understanding the benefits of the Uniform Thrift Savings Plan (TSP) and the importance of long term goals. In addition to mandatory unit training, a broad menu of classes is offered, such as checkbook management, personal financial management, credit report review and repair, car buying strategies, advice for first time home buyers, prevention of identity theft, and retirement planning. These full-spectrum proactive and responsive services can also be customized to meet the specific needs of an individual member or unit. For example, one workshop called "Money Talk" is designed to help military couples improve their communication about financial issues. Spouses are given valuable tools to conduct the "money talk" conversation so expectations of financial issues are addressed prior to a Servicemember's return from deployment, to ease reintegration and reduce stress. For military families stationed in Hawaii, this training is especially valuable, since the cost of living is approximately 30% higher than on the mainland. Relying on this expert advice, couples learn to plan a budget, develop a family spending plan, get or stay out of debt, and enhance their long-term financial health.

Question 7. Aside from these group lectures, how do individual soldiers seek counsel for their individual situations?

Response. Individuals may either request financial counseling directly or be referred by leadership. Appointments can be made directly to the nearest Personal Financial Management (PFM) office, such as the Army Family Readiness Program, the USAF Airmen and Family Readiness Center, the Navy and Marine Corps Fleet and Family Support Center, or a Joint Service provider, such as the Military Family Support Center at Joint Base Pearl Harbor-Hickam. At the local level, Servicemembers and their families have immediate access to PFM counselors to discuss their concerns, and may also attend classes, online webinars, and workshops to help meet their financial goals. Many installation programs have an active online presence through social media, augmenting their ability to share information and helpful resources like the Military Saves campaign or Military OneSource.

The Department also recognizes that financial readiness has a direct impact on our mission readiness, and that the promotion our PFM programs must be a leadership priority. The Military Services have created "train the trainer" courses for unit leaders to understand and leverage the tools available to promote, enhance, and maintain personal financial readiness. The Command Financial Non-Commissioned Officers Course (CFNCO), as one example, provides enlisted leaders with 40 hours of instruction about the key programs, individual counseling services, and referral procedures available to assist Soldiers with financial difficulties. CFNCO prepares NCOs to serve as the battalion commander's in-house advisor on personal financial readiness issues and local consumer affairs. Each battalion-sized element has a financially-savvy CFNCO who trains, organizes, implements and supervises the CFNCO program in the unit, and can refer individuals to PFMs and other resources, like legal assistance. The Commander's Referral Program, is another tool that Commanders and First Sergeants can use to deter families from relying on predatory leaders or high-interest credit, offering no-interest loans up to $2,500.

Moreover, military and family members may seek free, confidential, and professional legal assistance regarding civil law and consumer rights issues at DOD installations worldwide. While legal assistance attorneys usually cannot represent family members directly in court, they can refer eligible clients to civilian experts via the American Bar Association's Legal Assistance for Military Personnel (LAMP) program. Our legal experts also can report consumer complaints to the Consumer Financial Protection Bureau (CFPB), U.S. Department of Justice, and State Attorneys General for potential enforcement action against financial institutions for abusive practices.

Question 8. Furthermore, does the counseling provided vary to address the difficulties specific to each of these transitioning situations? For example, does it cover

23

financial obligations servicemembers have agreed to that don't involve loans but can still impact credit (i.e. a gym membership)?

Response. Yes. As a key element of our Family Readiness System, all Military Service Personal Financial Management (PFM) counselors are capable of providing advice tailored to the individual's concerns and community-specific issues. The one-on-one counseling services provided address a myriad of situations like the gym membership example mentioned above. As discussed, PFMs provide information and expert advice on a broad range of topics through a seminars, workshops, unit on-site visits, and one-on-one counseling.

Emphasis is placed on sound money management, check writing, debit card principles, proper use of credit, credit report review and repair, effective financial planning for deployment, transition and relocation assistance, insurance management, debt elimination strategies, investment strategies, retirement planning, benefits under the Servicemembers Civil Relief Act (SCRA), and the consequences of predatory lending. For example, financial readiness workshops offered at Fort Bragg in 2013 covered ''Budgeting for Babies,'' ''Marriage Money Matters'' and ''Money Management for Teens,'' among other issues affecting the community at large. This proactive, life-cycle approach ensures that PFMs can help individuals develop a personal financial spending plan, learn tips to stay out of debt, and smartly manage their money throughout their careers. Servicemembers and dependent family members may also consult military legal assistance attorneys for advice on these issues, such as one's protection against harassment from debt collectors under the Fair Debt Collection Practices Act, or how to refer a consumer fraud complaint to the Consumer Financial Protection Bureau.

The Department has developed financial readiness programs to promote financial literacy and sound planning over the entire course of a military member's career. This includes a broad umbrella of education and support services to assist military families in improving their financial well-being, financial self-sufficiency, and reducing financial stressors. Additionally, PFMs provide information and support concerning consumer awareness, consumer advocacy, and emergency financial assistance.

Question 9. How does the Defense Manpower Data Center (DMDC) system protect against identity theft, given that the system is open to anyone who submits a request?

Response. From April 1, 2012 through January 31, 2013, the Servicemembers Civil Relief Act (SCRA) Website responded to more than 600 million inquiries from financial institutions, creditors, landlords, etc., for the Active Duty status of an individual, and of those 600 million, over 56 million of those inquiries were for individuals who were current or former Servicemembers or their spouses. The 56 million inquiries represent approximately 6 million unique current or former Servicemembers and their spouses who were provided protection through the use of the enhanced SCRA Web site, 24 percent of which were on active duty on the date specified in the Web site inquiry. Additionally, the Department of Justice (DoJ) used the SCRA Web site and Defense Enrollment Eligibility Reporting Systems (DEERS) data in several lawsuits against financial institutions in which funds were returned to the affected Servicemembers.

Because the SCRA Web site is a public Web site (i.e., available to anyone with access to the Internet), and the information contained within it is sensitive in nature, the system includes several layers of protection of sensitive information. Creditors performing single-record checks must, for example, provide multiple data points in any query they make: last name and Social Security Number, or last name and date of birth. They receive in response only a data point that indicates whether the Servicemember was on active duty at the time requested.

DMDC has developed the SCRA Batch process to respond to requests coming from financial institutions. The SCRA Batch process requires that the institution have a Secure File Transfer Protocol (SFTP) site that can be accessed by the SCRA Batch process. The input files submitted shall contain all of the information required to check the active duty status of each person on a specified date in the file. The return batch file will contain all of the information originally provided, plus the additional information necessary to determine active duty status on the date of interest. Thus, when utilizing batch processing, creditors or financial institutions must provide all required data and receive in response only that data they supplied previously, plus information as to whether the Servicemember was on active duty on the date specified or within 367 days thereof. In other words, DMDC provides no additional sensitive or personal information which the creditor or financial institution does not already possess and provide in their inquiry regarding the Servicemember.

Chairman SANDERS. Colonel, thank you very much.
Mr. Halperin.

STATEMENT OF ERIC HALPERIN, SPECIAL COUNSEL FOR FAIR LENDING, CIVIL RIGHTS DIVISION, U.S. DEPARTMENT OF JUSTICE

Mr. HALPERIN. Good morning, Chairman Sanders, Senator Boozman, and Members of the Committee. Thank you for holding this hearing on preserving the rights of servicemembers, veterans, and their families in the financial marketplace. It is a privilege to speak with you today about our shared priority of protecting the rights of our men and women in uniform.

Over the past 4 years, the Department of Justice has made enforcement of the Servicemember Civil Relief Act, or SCRA, a top priority. I am pleased to share with you today some of the recent successes we have had in ensuring that servicemembers' homes and credit are protected while they serve our Nation. We have also learned some important lessons from our enforcement efforts and have been reviewing ways to strengthen the SCRA.

The Civil Rights Division enforces several laws designed to protect the rights of members of the military, one of which is the SCRA. The SCRA's protections are important because servicemembers should not have to worry that their family could lose their home while they are on deployment, or that their cars will be repossessed while they are on the front lines overseas, or suffer financial penalties from landlords because they have been ordered to move to a different duty station.

Members of the military who made great personal sacrifices on behalf of this country should not be required to transition to civilian life only to find their credit ruined and their home sold off. That is why, over the past 4 years, the Department has filed more SCRA enforcement actions than ever before.

For example, during one of our investigations we discovered a servicemember who was severely injured by an improvised explosive device while serving in Iraq, breaking his back and causing Traumatic Brain Injury. His loan servicer foreclosed on him improperly, despite receiving notice on multiple occasions that he was serving in Iraq. That should never happen.

Behind our enforcement actions are countless other stories of hardship experienced by servicemembers and their families as a result of failures of lenders and servicers to comply with the law. In 2012, the Division reached settlements with the Nation's five largest mortgage loan servicers who agreed to compensate all servicemembers they improperly foreclosed on or charged unlawfully high interest rates.

This settlement, along with three other wrongful foreclosure settlements reached by the Division in 2011 and 2012 will ensure that the vast majority of foreclosures against servicemembers will be subject to court-ordered review.

Most servicemembers illegally foreclosed on will receive $125,000 plus any equity lost in their home. In addition, these settlements require servicers to submit their SCRA policies and procedures to the Department for review and approval, and to submit to ongoing monitoring by the Department.

As you know, the SCRA's protections extend well beyond mortgages. In July 2012, we resolved our complaint against Capital One and filed one of the most comprehensive SCRA settlements ever obtained by the Government agency or any private party. The case involved allegations of a variety of violations, including wrongful foreclosures, improper repossessions of motor vehicles, wrongful court judgments, and improper denials of the 6 percent interest rate that the SCRA guarantees to servicemembers on pre-service credit card and other loans.

As a result of our enforcement over the last 4 years, servicers and lenders are required to pay more than $50 million in monetary relief to servicemembers and that number will increase once the foreclosure reviews of the five largest servicers are completed.

The Civil Rights Division enforcement actions have addressed the full range of protections under the SCRA, including a number of cases that do not involve the financial services industry, such as wrongful charges by landlords. In enforcing the SCRA, we have worked closely with our Federal and State partners.

The Department of Defense has been invaluable to our enforcement efforts, especially our ability to bring large pattern and practice cases, and the CFPB has been a critical source of information about the financial challenges facing servicemembers and potential SCRA violations in the marketplace.

While vigorous enforcement of the SCRA is critical, we recognize that to maximize compliance with the law, we also need to engage at outreach and education to industry and the military community to inform people of their rights and responsibilities. That is why the Department engages directly in outreach, as do our partners at other agencies.

Although we have achieved great successes on behalf of servicemembers, we have also identified ways that the SCRA could be strengthened. In September 2011, the Administration formally transmitted to Congress a package of proposals for strengthening all three servicemember civil rights statutes that the Division enforces, including the SCRA.

We were gratified to see that this Committee considered many of our proposals in the last Congress. We are actively considering additional improvements and we look forward to working with you in this Congress to strengthen the SCRA, and we hope to see these proposals enacted into law.

Our recommendations include codifying the rule that a party seeing a default judgment against a servicemember must check the Department of Defense records to determine whether the servicemember is on active duty, and granting the Department the authority to compel the production of existing documents during our SCRA investigations.

The Department appreciates the opportunity to report on the SCRA and we stand ready to work with the Committee in strengthening this important law. Thank you for the opportunity to testify today and I look forward to answering your questions.

[The prepared statement of Mr. Halperin follows:]

PREPARED STATEMENT OF ERIC HALPERIN, ACTING DEPUTY ASSISTANT ATTORNEY GENERAL, CIVIL RIGHTS DIVISION, U.S. DEPARTMENT OF JUSTICE

Good morning, Chairman Sanders, Ranking Member Burr, and Members of the Committee. Thank you for holding this hearing on preserving the rights of servicemembers, veterans and their families in the financial marketplace. It is a privilege to speak with you today about our shared priority of protecting the rights of our men and women in uniform.

Over the past four years, the Department of Justice has made enforcement of the Servicemembers Civil Relief Act (SCRA) a top priority. I am pleased to share with you today some of the recent successes we have had in working with the Department of Defense and the Office of Servicemember Affairs at the Consumer Financial Protection Bureau to ensure that servicemembers' homes and credit are protected while they serve our Nation. We have also learned some important lessons from our enforcement efforts over recent years and have been reviewing ways this law could be amended to better protect the rights of servicemembers.

I. SCRA ENFORCEMENT ACCOMPLISHMENTS

The Civil Rights Division enforces several laws designed to protect the rights of members of the military, including the SCRA which provides a wide-range of protections. Among other protections, the SCRA postpones, suspends, terminates, or reduces the amount of certain consumer debt obligations for active duty members of the Armed Forces, so that they can focus their full attention on their military responsibilities without adverse consequences for themselves or their families. Among these protections are: (1) a prohibition on foreclosure of a servicemember's property without first getting approval from the court if the servicemember obtained the loan prior to entering military service, (2) a prohibition on foreclosure of an active duty servicemember's property through a default judgment without first filing an affidavit alerting the court to the servicemember's military status, and (3) the right of a servicemember to have his or her interest rate lowered to six percent on debt that was incurred before entering military service.

These protections are in place because servicemembers should not have to worry—that their cars will be repossessed while they are on the front lines overseas, that they could lose their home, or that their spouses and children will be evicted while they are on deployment.

Enforcing these rights has been a top priority of the Division under the leadership of Attorney General Holder and former Assistant Attorney General Perez. Members of the military who have made great personal sacrifices on behalf of this country should not be required to transition to civilian life only to find their credit ruined and their homes foreclosed on and sold. In enforcing the SCRA, we have worked closely with our Federal and state partners. The Department of Defense has been invaluable to our enforcement efforts, especially our ability to bring large pattern or practice cases, and the CFPB has been an important source of information about the financial challenges facing servicemembers.

A. Wrongful Foreclosure Cases

In 2011, we reached two multi-million dollar settlements on behalf of servicemembers whose homes had been foreclosed on without court orders while they were on active duty or shortly after they had returned from active duty. The first settlement was for over $38 million with Bank of America. The Bank of America case began with a referral from the United States Marine Corps on behalf of a servicemember who was deployed to Iraq. Bank of America was scheduled to sell that servicemember's home at a trustee's sale in three days, even though the bank had already received a copy of his military orders. In the course of our investigation and settlement negotiations, the Department found that 309 servicemembers' homes were illegally foreclosed on between 2006 and 2010. Under the consent decree, Bank of America will pay each victim a minimum of $116,785, plus compensation for any equity lost with interest.

Under our second settlement, Saxon Mortgage Services Inc. is in the process of paying out over $2.5 million to 19 servicemembers whose homes were unlawfully foreclosed upon between 2006 and 2010. Each servicemember will receive a minimum of $130,555, plus compensation for any equity lost with interest.

Under both settlements, the banks have agreed not to pursue any remaining amounts owed under the mortgages; to take steps to remedy negative credit reporting; and to implement enhanced measures, including monitoring, training, and checking loans against the Defense Manpower Data Center's SCRA database during the foreclosure process.

In February 2012, we filed consent orders with Bank of America, JPMorgan Chase & Co., Wells Fargo & Company, Citigroup Inc., and Ally Financial, Inc. (formerly GMAC) in *United States, et al., v. Bank of America Corp., et al.* (D.D.C.). These consent orders are known as "the National Mortgage Settlement," which was reached by the United States, 49 state attorneys general, the District of Columbia and the five servicers in 2012. Under these agreements, loans serviced by the Nation's five largest mortgage loan servicers are being reviewed to find all servicemembers foreclosed on either judicially or non-judicially in violation of the SCRA since 2006, and to find all servicemembers unlawfully charged interest in excess of six percent on their mortgages since 2008. As a result of these settlements, combined with the Department's other SCRA settlements, the vast majority of all foreclosures against servicemembers are now subject to court-ordered review.

Under the National Mortgage Settlement, most servicemembers wrongly foreclosed on will receive $125,000 plus any lost equity with interest. For the foreclosure violations that took place in 2009 and 2010, the Justice Department is coordinating with the Office of the Comptroller of the Currency and the Federal Reserve Board, which are conducting separate reviews of 12 mortgage servicers under the Independent Foreclosure Review process.

Under the National Mortgage Settlement, Servicemembers who were denied a required reduction to a six percent interest rate will also receive a minimum of four times the amount wrongfully charged in excess of six percent. The financial compensation to servicemembers provided by the settlement is in addition to the $25 billion in relief the settlement provides to homeowners based on the servicers' illegal mortgage loan servicing practices.

Behind each of these settlements are stories of servicemembers who have made great sacrifices for our country, only to have their rights violated at home. For example, we encountered a case involving a servicemember who was severely injured by an Improvised Explosive Device while serving in Iraq, breaking his back and causing Traumatic Brain Injury. The servicer foreclosed on him, despite receiving notice on multiple occasions that he was serving in Iraq. He returned to the United States in a wheelchair with the prognosis that he would never walk again. He spent two years in recovery, during which time he re-learned how to walk and eventually run; however, he still suffers from the impact of Traumatic Brain Injury. Under our settlement, the servicemember received $130,651 and is eligible to have his credit report corrected to reflect that the foreclosure was not valid.

In another case, we encountered a victim who suffers from Post-Traumatic Distress Syndrome after a tour in Iraq in 2003–2004. Consequently, he regularly receives counseling and takes medication to address his nightmares and nervous condition. In an attempt to avoid foreclosure on his home, he notified the servicer of his active duty status and provided copies of his orders. However, the servicer foreclosed on him twice despite notice of his protected status.

B. Wrongful Foreclosures, Repossessions and Court Judgments; Improper Denials of Six Percent Interest Rate

In July 2012, we filed and settled *United States* v. *Capital One, N.A.* (E.D. Va.), one of the most comprehensive SCRA settlements ever obtained by a government agency or any private party under the SCRA. Under the consent order, Capital One agreed to pay more than $15 million in monetary relief to resolve allegations of a variety of SCRA violations, including wrongful foreclosures, improper repossessions of motor vehicles, wrongful court judgments, improper denials of the six percent interest rate that the SCRA guarantees to servicemembers on pre-service credit card and other loans, and insufficient six percent benefits granted on credit cards, car loans and other types of accounts. The agreement requires Capital One to pay approximately $7 million in damages to servicemembers for SCRA violations, including at least $125,000 plus compensation for any lost equity (with interest) to each servicemember whose home was unlawfully foreclosed upon, and at least $10,000 plus compensation for any lost equity (with interest) to each servicemember whose motor vehicle was unlawfully repossessed. In addition, the agreement required Capital One to create a $5 million fund to compensate servicemembers who did not receive the appropriate amount of SCRA benefits after requesting a reduction to a six percent interest rate on their credit card accounts, motor vehicle finance loans, and consumer loans. Approximately $3 million of this fund was used as payments to servicemembers. The remaining approximately $2 million has been donated by Capital One to military emergency aid societies. Thousands of servicemembers who were victims of Capital One's unfair lending practices will be identified and compensated, with no action required on their part, for loans dating back to July 15, 2006, and those whose credit scores were damaged because Capital One violated the SCRA will have their credit scores repaired.

II. COMMENTS ON PENDING LEGISLATION

Through our enforcement work, we have achieved great successes on behalf of servicemembers, but we have also identified ways that the SCRA could be strengthened to better protect the rights of servicemembers. In September 2011, the Administration formally transmitted to Congress a package of proposals for strengthening all three statutes enforced by the Civil Rights Division that protect the rights of servicemembers and their families, including the SCRA,[1] and we are eager to work with the Committee on these proposals. We were pleased that, last Congress, then-Chairwoman Senator Patty Murray included many of our proposals in S. 2299, the "Servicemembers Rights Enforcement Improvement Act."

These proposals, if passed, would:

• Double the amount of civil penalties currently available under the SCRA, to $110,000 for a first violation and $220,000 for subsequent violations;

• Codify the rule that a party seeking a default judgment against a servicemember must check Department of Defense records to determine whether the servicemember is on active duty;

• Clarify retroactive application of provisions establishing a private right of action and the authority of the Attorney General to enforce the SCRA; and

• Grant civil investigative demand authority to the Attorney General to compel the production of existing documents in SCRA investigations.

When Congress amended the SCRA to provide for civil penalties in 2010, it used the amounts authorized under the Fair Housing Amendments Act. These amounts, however, have not been adjusted for inflation or for any other reason since 1999. Some violations of the SCRA involve small monetary amounts, making the civil penalty critical to ensuring compliance.

We urge the Committee to amend the SCRA's affidavit requirement, which provides that a party seeking foreclosure or other default judgment against a servicemember must first file with the court an affidavit stating whether or not the servicemember is in military service, to clarify that such requirement includes the obligation to take reasonable steps to determine the servicemember's military status. Such steps would include, but are not limited to, searching available Department of Defense records. The amendment would simply codify what several courts have already held.

We also urge the Committee to amend the SCRA to clarify that the private right of action and the Attorney General's authority to enforce the SCRA, which were made explicit in the Veterans' Benefits Act of 2010, apply retroactively to violations occurring before the date of enactment of that Act. This would be consistent with the Department's litigating position and with the recent decisions of the United States Court of Appeals for the Fourth Circuit, and would ensure that the SCRA rights of all servicemembers can be vindicated.

Finally, the Department urges the Committee to amend the SCRA to provide the Attorney General with civil investigative demand (CID) authority. The Department of Justice has no pre-suit investigative authority under the SCRA, and must rely on voluntary cooperation from the subjects of our investigations. Greater investigative authority would strengthen the Department's ability to enforce the SCRA, especially through pattern or practice suits.

In addition, the Administration has proposed as part of the FY 2014 National Defense Authorization Act to give the Department the ability to bring enforcement actions under the Military Lending Act (MLA) if violations of that Act constitute a pattern or practice or raise an issue of public importance. This is analogous to the Department's enforcement authority under the SCRA and would allow for more efficient and effective law enforcement, especially when actors are engaged in conduct that potentially violates both the MLA and the SCRA.

We will continue to work with Congress to identify areas in which additional legislative changes would improve enforcement of the SCRA and the MLA, which also extends vital economic protections to our servicemembers, and anticipate advancing additional legislative proposals this Congress.

III. LOOKING FORWARD

The Department appreciates the opportunity to report on our accomplishments in enforcing the SCRA, and to comment on our legislative proposals to strengthen the SCRA. We stand ready to work with the Committee in strengthening this important law that protects the rights of our servicemembers.

---

[1] The other two statutes are the Uniformed Services Employment and Reemployment Rights Act (USERRA) and Uniformed and Overseas Citizens Absentee Voting Act (UOCAVA).

Thank you for the opportunity to testify today, and I look forward to answering your questions.

———

RESPONSE TO POSTHEARING QUESTIONS SUBMITTED BY HON. BERNARD SANDERS TO ERIC HALPERIN, SPECIAL COUNSEL FOR FAIR LENDING, CIVIL RIGHTS DIVISION, U.S. DEPARTMENT OF JUSTICE

1. **Has the Department ever sought or has a court ever imposed the civil penalties allowed under the Servicemembers Civil Relief Act? If yes, please provide a brief description of or a citation to the case(s).**

Response:

The Department of Justice (DOJ) was first given the authority to seek civil penalties under the Servicemembers Civil Relief Act (SCRA) in the Veterans' Benefits Act of 2010, which was enacted on October 13, 2010.

To date, the Department has sought and obtained a civil penalty under the SCRA in two cases. In *United States v. Capital One, N.A.*, Case 1:12-cv-00828-JCC-IDD (E.D. Va.), the consent decree, which was entered by the court on July 27, 2012, required the defendants to pay $55,000 to the United States Treasury, which is the maximum civil penalty pursuant to 50 U.S.C. App. § 597(b)(3). This amount has been paid. In *United States v. Sallie Mae* (D. Del.), the consent decree also required the payment of a $55,000 civil penalty. This consent decree was filed on May 13, 2014, and has not yet been ruled on by the court.

In future cases alleging violations of the SCRA that occurred after the enactment of the Veterans' Benefits Act, the Department expects to seek civil penalties in all appropriate cases.

2. **Has the Department ever sought or has a court ever imposed the criminal penalties allowed under the Servicemembers Civil Relief Act? If yes, please provide a brief description of or a citation to the case(s).**

Response:

The Department does not track cases in which criminal penalties were imposed under the SCRA, but the criminal penalty provisions are useful both in practice and as a deterrent. An example of a case involving a violation of SCRA's criminal penalties is *United States v. Carl Ralph Nuss* in the Northern District of Alabama. Mr. Nuss was sentenced to 36 months of probation and made restitution in the amount of $7,310.00.[1] In a 2008 case, a U.S. Magistrate Judge, at the government's request, departed upward for "extreme conduct" based on the defendant's having

---

[1] *See* http://www.justice.gov/usao/aln/News/June%202013/June%2027,%202013%20Cullman%20Car%20Dealer.html.

evicted the pregnant wife of an absent servicemember with her two young children in the middle of winter and never returning their personal property to them. Noting that the crime was only "a misdemeanor, but it's a pretty horrendous one," the court sentenced the defendant to 6 months of imprisonment and ordered him to pay $15,300 in restitution. The restitution order (the only issue subject to the appeal) was affirmed by the district court in *United States v. McLeod*, 2008 WL 114789 (W.D. Mich. Jan. 9, 2008).

3. **For each of the three major settlements (BAC Home Loans Servicing LP, Saxon Mortgage Servicing, Inc. and Capital One, N.A.) reached by the Department as a result of violations of the Servicemembers Civil Relief Act, please provide the status of the provision of the relief required by these settlements. Please provide information, to date, on how many individuals have received the relief required by the settlements, the amount of such relief, and when DoJ anticipates compliance with the settlement agreements will be complete.**

Response:

On May 26, 2011, the United States filed a complaint and consent order in *United States v. BAC Home Loans Servicing, LP f/k/a Countrywide Home Loans Servicing, LP* (C.D. Cal.). The complaint alleged that Countrywide foreclosed without court orders on the pre-service residential mortgages of servicemembers in states that allowed for non-judicial foreclosure. We have identified 306 servicemembers whose mortgages were foreclosed on in violation of the SCRA from January 1, 2006 to December 31, 2010. Under the consent order, Bank of America (BAC)/Countrywide will be required to pay more than $38 million in compensation. Moreover, Countrywide will not pursue any remaining amount owed by the servicemembers and must take steps to remedy negative credit reporting directly resulting from Countrywide's improper foreclosures. The consent order also requires BAC/Countrywide to set up a monitoring program to test for effective compliance with the SCRA, give SCRA training to employees who provide customer service to servicemembers or who have significant involvement in any aspect of the mortgage foreclosure process and perform systematic checks of the Defense Manpower Data Center's SCRA database during the foreclosure process.

Notices have been sent to all 306 servicemembers and, to date, 253 have responded and been paid a total of more than $31 million. We are continuing our efforts to secure responses from the remaining servicemembers.

On May 26, 2011, the United States filed a complaint and the court entered a consent order in *United States v. Saxon Mortgage Services, Inc.* (N.D. Tex.). The complaint alleged that Saxon foreclosed without court orders on the pre-service residential mortgages of servicemembers in states that allowed for non-judicial foreclosure. We have identified 19 servicemembers who were foreclosed in violation of the SCRA from January 1, 2006 to December 31, 2010. Under the consent order, Saxon was required to pay more than $2.5 million in compensation. In addition, Saxon agreed to non-monetary relief similar to the relief in the BAC/Countrywide case, which is described above. In the Saxon case, all nineteen of the victims have been paid.

On July 26, 2012, the United States filed a complaint in *United States v. Capital One, N.A.* (E.D. Va.), alleging that Capital One engaged in a wide range of conduct that violated the SCRA, including wrongful foreclosures, improper repossessions of motor vehicles, wrongful court judgments, improper denials of the 6% interest rate on credit card and car loans, and insufficient 6% benefits granted on credit cards, car loans, and other types of accounts. A proposed consent order was filed with the complaint and was entered by the court on July 27, 2012. This case is one of the most comprehensive ever obtained by a government agency or any private party under the SCRA. The consent order requires Capital One to pay at least $125,000 in compensation plus compensation for any lost equity (with interest) to each servicemember whose home was unlawfully foreclosed upon, and at least $10,000 plus compensation for any lost equity (with interest) to each servicemember whose motor vehicle was unlawfully repossessed. To date, Capital One has issued over 41,000 checks totaling over $12 million to individuals eligible for compensation under the consent order. On February 1, 2013, Capital One donated $1,970,336 to military aid societies. Total potential liability in this case exceeds $15 million.

In all three of these cases, DOJ has reviewed and provided comments on the servicers' modified SCRA policies, procedures and training programs, to minimize the chances that SCRA violations will occur in the future. Also in all three cases, servicemembers determined to have been victims have received not only monetary compensation but also credit repair.

4. **Please provide the status of the audits, including the number of known violations, required by the National Mortgage Settlement to identify violations of the Servicemembers Civil Relief Act? In addition, please provide an analysis, to date, of the servicers' compliance with the Servicemembers Civil Relief Act terms of the settlement agreements.**

Response:

On March 12, 2012, the United States, 49 states and the District of Columbia filed a complaint and five proposed consent orders in *United States v. Bank of America Corp., Citibank, NA, JPMorgan Chase & Co., Ally Financial, Inc. and Wells Fargo & Co.* (D.D.C.). Under the consent orders, which were entered by the court on April 4, 2012, the nation's five largest mortgage loan servicers are conducting reviews to determine whether any servicemembers have been foreclosed on either judicially or non-judicially in violation of the SCRA since 2006. Three of the five servicers are also conducting reviews to determine whether servicemembers have been unlawfully charged interest in excess of six percent on their mortgages since 2008. Foreclosure victims identified through these reviews will be compensated a minimum of $125,000 each plus any lost equity with interest. Victims of violations of the SCRA's 6% interest rate cap identified through these reviews will be compensated by the amount wrongfully charged in excess of 6%, plus triple the amount refunded, or $500, whichever is larger. All five servicers agreed to numerous other measures, including SCRA training for employees and agents and developing SCRA policies and procedures to ensure compliance with the SCRA in the future. The servicers will also repair any negative credit report entries related to the allegedly wrongful foreclosures and will not pursue any remaining amounts owed under the mortgages.

We are working diligently to complete a comprehensive review that will identify all potential victims as soon as possible. We have processed more than 3.4 million foreclosures through the Department of Defense database and from that group narrowed it down to the servicemembers whose files are getting a careful review to determine whether their rights may have been violated. We expect that payments to servicemembers who were foreclosure victims will begin to go out in the fall of 2014. The servicers are in substantial compliance with the decree with regard to the provision of policies and procedures for DOJ review.

RESPONSE TO POSTHEARING QUESTIONS SUBMITTED BY HON. JOHN D. ROCKEFELLER IV TO ERIC HALPERIN, SPECIAL COUNSEL FOR FAIR LENDING, CIVIL RIGHTS DIVISION, U.S. DEPARTMENT OF JUSTICE

5. I sincerely appreciate your testimony about the settlements that the Department of Justice has secured on behalf of servicemembers for violations of the Servicemembers Civil Relief Act, and I am glad that the Department of Justice has taken these matters so seriously. However, I am interested in finding out about how this relief is actually getting out to servicemembers. What efforts are being made to identify these families and make sure that they are being compensated in proportion to the hardships and wrongdoing they suffered? Can you describe to me how the relief that has been secured on behalf of these families is making its way into their hands in a timely and appropriate way?

Response:

Please refer to the responses to Questions 3 and 4, above.

————

RESPONSE TO POSTHEARING QUESTIONS SUBMITTED BY HON. MAZIE HIRONO TO ERIC HALPERIN, SPECIAL COUNSEL FOR FAIR LENDING, CIVIL RIGHTS DIVISION, U.S. DEPARTMENT OF JUSTICE

6. Would legislation similar to Florida's Military Protection Act at the federal level be practical?

Response:

The Department supports improvements to federal laws that protect servicemembers from financial abuse, including the SCRA and the Military Lending Act. In addition, although we have not had an opportunity to review state statutes, the Department would be happy to provide technical assistance on any proposals modeled after Florida's Military Protection Act.

7. You mention in your testimony that during the course of your investigation and settlement negotiations, 309 cases of illegally foreclosed homes were discovered. Were these reported beforehand and tracked alongside the original incidents or were these revealed?

Response:

These foreclosures were identified during the review conducted pursuant to the consent order.

8. Given these cases above, what is your assessment of effectiveness of the Military One Source (MOS) program, and how could it be improved?

Response:

Military One Source is an important source of information for servicemembers and their families to use to advocate for their rights under the SCRA. However, some servicemembers are unable to secure their rights even when they contact their financial institutions and are aware of the protections under the SCRA. That is why it is essential to complement education to servicemembers with outreach to industry stakeholders and a vigorous enforcement program.

Chairman SANDERS. Thank you all very much. We have been joined by Senator Hirono. I just learned that we are going to have votes at 10:55, so we are going to take questions now, move to the next panel, and we will be out of here by that time.

Let me start with you, Mrs. Petraeus. A law only good if people know about it. So, we can have the best laws in the world, but if people do not know about it, it does not do us all that much good. In your judgment, do the men and women who serve in the military, in fact, know what protections they have?

Ms. PETRAEUS. Well, I think that might be a question that Colonel Kantwill could answer better. I can tell you that some of the people who answer the phone at loan servicers do not know the law and do not apply it properly. We continue to have real concerns about what we have seen in that area. We just saw a complaint come in this past week where someone told a servicemember that in order to be eligible for the SCRA, they needed to have been on active duty on or after September 11, 2001, which, of course, was completely incorrect.

So, I think there is an awareness of the law, but again, people are misapplying its provisions, giving out wrong information. I think the Department of Defense—I cannot speak for them, but I think they are trying hard to raise awareness about that among servicemembers before they go onto active duty so they know what they have.

Many of them enter the military with loans, student loans, some with mortgages, some with other debt, and it is important that they know that they can reduce—ask to have that interest rate reduced.

Chairman SANDERS. Let me ask Colonel Kantwill that same question, because that is within your jurisdiction. Are we doing a decent job so that members of the military know what their rights are?

Colonel KANTWILL. I think we are, sir, and I think we are doing a much, much better in recent years. And I would answer that in two parts, if I may. On the active duty side of the house, the legal community has been absolutely essential in our outreach programs. We now have legal folks who are briefing folks when they reach the installation level, when they leave the installation, in-processing and out-processing, as it were.

In pre-deployment briefings and in post-deployment briefings as well, and we found that that has been very, very effective.

Chairman SANDERS. And that information is getting back to the folks at home as well so the spouse knows?

Colonel KANTWILL. Absolutely, sir. We have family support groups and other sort of mechanisms on the installations that invite the family support groups in, the individual family members as well. They get the same briefings. Preventive law articles appear in the community newspapers, on the community channels on the installations, et cetera. The news gets out very, very well.

A bigger challenge has been on the Reserve component side of the house, admittedly, particularly when we have got a smaller window of boots-on-the-ground time, as you know well. That has pushed into the home station training a lot more that we were able to do at the mobilization stations in the past. But once again, I think we have met that challenge, and we have been able to do it largely through the legal community, both in pre-mobilization briefings and in post-mobilization briefings, and through the use of the legal assets that are habitually assigned to those organizations in regard to——

Chairman SANDERS. Let me get to Mr. Halperin. You indicated in your testimony a number of the largest financial institutions in this country have been involved in ripping off men and women in the Armed Forces. Have we been aggressive in going after these financial institutions? Are you happy with the settlement that was reached?

Mr. HALPERIN. The settlement we reached with the five largest financial institutions, we think, is a fair, good, strong settlement on several fronts. So, on front, in terms of compensating our servicemembers, it ensures that every single servicemember who was improperly foreclosed on between 2006 and April 2012 will be compensated at a minimum level of $125,000.

And there is no cap on that. The financial firms that we reached a settlement with agreed to compensate every single person we found. There is no limitation.

Chairman SANDERS. Are there any criminal penalties involved here?

Mr. HALPERIN. This settlement was a civil settlement. The Civil Rights Division enforces the civil provisions of the SCRA. The criminal provisions are enforced by our colleagues in the Criminal Division and at U.S. Attorney's offices. And although there is no criminal element of this civil settlement, I do know that our colleagues have brought criminal indictments in other cases and I would be happy to have them provide that information to you.

Chairman SANDERS. Are you reasonably confident that the banks will end this type of behavior?

Mr. HALPERIN. Well, the second component of the settlement is the going-forward piece, which is vitally important to ensuring compliance going forward. So, under the settlement, all their policies and procedures around the SCRA needed to be submitted to us and were approved by us. Then the settlement includes, for a period of years, direct monitoring by the Civil Rights Division, and provisions in place that, in the event any servicemember's SCRA rights are violated, automatic remedies kick in.

Hopefully, the goal of those compliance policies is, if for some reason anyone slips through the cracks, it is caught quickly and quick enough so the foreclosure does not happen, because money is good, but it is not an adequate remedy to replacing someone's home.

Chairman SANDERS. Thank you. Senator Boozman, Senator Hirono, I understand, has to preside at 10:30. Is that the case? Would you mind if she jumped the line?

Senator BOOZMAN. Not at all.

Chairman SANDERS. Senator Hirono.

STATEMENT OF HON. MAZIE HIRONO, U.S. SENATOR FROM HAWAII

Senator HIRONO. Thank you, Mr Chairman, and thank you, Senator Boozman. I want to commend all of you for your commitment in helping our servicemembers, veterans and their families because they are very much, based on the testimony and the information

I get from the calls, that my office gets, that they are often targeted for all kinds of, whatever it is called, predatory practices.

Ms. Petraeus, I note in your testimony that you made reference to a Florida law that provided enhanced protections against various kinds of practices that target veterans and servicemembers, enhanced unfair trade practice kind of laws. Do you consider that kind of an approach effective at the State level?

Ms. PETRAEUS. I think the States can certainly build on and enhance what is done here at the Federal level. In this case, the State of Florida chose to provide extra penalties to those who ripped off veterans, and it also put the veterans who had been injured ahead of others in the queue for any damages that resulted from the suits. So, I think it can enhance protection. So, yes, a multifaceted approach like that is great.

Senator HIRONO. Have other States followed suit with these kinds of enhanced protective laws?

Ms. PETRAEUS. I think there are a number of them. I would have to do some research to specify, but there are many States that, I think, have real concern for the military families that live and work there and have provided extra protections for them.

Senator HIRONO. Certainly, Hawaii is a State where there is a huge military presence as well as many veterans.

I want to focus on the educational parts, because that is really where a lot of abuses occur. There is the 90/10 Rule. You are very familiar, all of you, with the fact that for-profit colleges are restricted from receiving more than 90 percent of their revenues from Federal sources, but 10 percent can come from those receiving or using G.I. benefits. Do you consider that a loophole that should be closed?

Ms. PETRAEUS. I think it provides a real incentive to chase after servicemembers and use unscrupulous tactics to sign them up. And I mentioned in my statement one I heard about from a VA representative in Nevada who was doing rehab for vets with brain injuries and basically was appalled at the tactics where they were being pursued to sign up, not only for undergrad degrees, but master's degrees.

Senator HIRONO. So, if we pursue a remedy such as requiring that the G.I. Bill loans be included in the 90 percent, that would take away the incentive for some of these bad actors from targeting veterans?

Ms. PETRAEUS. Yes, I think it would remove some of the incentive that is there now.

Senator HIRONO. Would the other panel members agree that that might be a fruitful approach?

Colonel KANTWILL. That is a bit outside of my purview, ma'am, but I can tell you that the Department is absolutely committed to protecting our servicemembers in every respect, and we would be happy to work with the Congress in this regard.

Mr. HALPERIN. Yes, Senator, that is also outside of our purview under the SCRA. But I will note that under the SCRA, we are concerned with loans that are taken out while not on active duty, and then when someone becomes activated whether they get the full benefits of the 6 percent reduction when they request it. And we do have active investigations in that area, looking into a failure to provide servicemembers the full benefits under SCRA.

Senator HIRONO. So, even if these areas are not within your purview, you do collaborate and work together so that we are all going to the same goal of protecting our active duty servicemembers and veterans and their families. And with that, I want to thank the Chair and Senator Boozman. Thank you so much.

Chairman SANDERS. Thank you, Senator Hirono. Senator Boozman, I thank you very much for your courtesy.

Senator BOOZMAN. Thank you all so much for being here and we really do appreciate your advocacy and hard work, again, protecting our servicemembers.

Colonel Kantwill, you mentioned that things seem to be going well as far as the education process. Do we have any metrics in place that we could perhaps measure that to make sure that rather than just being anecdotal evidence, that we really do know what is going on?

Colonel KANTWILL. I can certainly take that back, sir, and see if we can provide some metrics for you. I can tell you that we do have indications such as the Military Saves campaign, which we have unprecedented participation in the past couple of years, are indicative of that, but we will be happy to come back to the Committee with more specific information. Thank you.

[The information requested during the hearing follows:]

RESPONSE TO REQUEST ARISING DURING THE HEARING BY HON. JOHN BOOZMAN TO COL. PAUL KANTWILL, DIRECTOR OF LEGAL POLICY, OFFICE OF THE UNDERSECRETARY FOR PERSONNEL AND READINESS, U.S. DEPARTMENT OF DEFENSE

The financial readiness of servicemembers and their families is a priority for the Department of Defense, as we recognize this issue has a direct impact on our mission readiness. Our efforts, therefore, are geared toward increasing the financial literacy of military families, and ensuring they know the resources available through our full-spectrum Family Readiness System programs. The Department is currently preparing a large-scale, multifaceted, and multi-year evaluation project to measure outcomes on DOD-wide family support programs, as well as developing a full portfolio of performance measures. This includes the Family Readiness Program Evaluation Plan Development Project, in collaboration with Penn State University, as well as a systematic review of Existing Personal Finance Data (DMDC Status of Force Surveys). The DOD has also increased it support partnerships through official Memorandums of Understanding (MOU) with Federal and non-profit agencies to leverage their expertise in promoting financial readiness. At this early stage, we can report several positive indicators that we are moving in the right direction in developing a military command climate and overall culture that supports prudent financial behavior through financial literacy education and counseling.

In addition to mandatory training for all entry-level Servicemembers, we are seeing increased participation by members and their families in our voluntary classes, workshops, and one-one financial planning and counseling services. In 2013 alone, our PFMs provided over 34,867 briefings to a total of 872,187 participants, and provided individual counseling to 1,828,299 individuals, including 161,992 extended contacts. Across the Services, our knowledgeable, well-trained and experienced teams of social workers, educators and specialists presently provide assistance and community-based support to military families on everything from money management, check writing, credit report review and repair, financial planning for deployments, debt elimination, investment strategies, retirement planning and transition assistance. This translates into more financially-savvy, less-stressed military families, who are able to proactively develop financial spending plans, manage debt, invest wisely, and save for retirement.

Another key metric we observe is the quarterly participation in the Thrift Savings Program (TSP) data by Service and rank. Due to entry-level briefings, as well as command support, we continue to see a gradual uptick in participation, particularly in the Navy, which now reports that approximately 47 percent of its officers and

56 percent of its enlisted members have elected to participate in TSP, as part of their long-term savings plan.

The "Military Saves" campaign, now in its seventh year, continues to see unprecedented participation. Co-sponsored by the Consumer Federation of America and the Department of Defense, this program has now become an integral part of our comprehensive Financial Readiness Campaign. This past year alone, Military Saves reached 137,392 servicemembers and families reached directly by installation efforts, along with another 163,000 through Facebook, 1.6 million Twitter impressions, 35,000 visits to MilitarySaves.org. Over 29,307 new individuals took the Military Saves pledge in 2013 to "build wealth, not debt," while encouraging others to do the same. As led by "our boots on the ground" PFMs, the Department continues to develop a military command climate and overall culture that supports prudent financial behavior through financial literacy education and counseling.

We have also sought to identify key trends through scientific surveys, such as the Military Family Life Project (MFLP), using a representative sample of the military population, including military spouses. In the 2010–2011 MFLP surveys, approximately 59 percent of spouses reported being comfortable about their financial condition, while 25 percent reported feeling less comfortable, and while 16 percent reported they were uncomfortable about their financial condition. These numbers remained consistent in the 2011 MFLP. We will continue to track these important indicators to ensure our comprehensive financial readiness programs are responsive to, and supportive of the needs and concerns of military families.

Furthermore, we have observed recent upward trends in savings habits in all career fields. As indicated by our 2011 MFLP survey (Figure 1.1), 66 percent of total military members now report having $500.00 or more in emergency savings, and 64 percent save regularly by putting aside money per month. For our entry level and most junior personnel, this breaks down to 45 percent having $500.00 or more in emergency savings, and 51 percent with continued savings. These are positive signs as we continue to enrich the financial readiness of our Total Force.

FIGURE 1.1

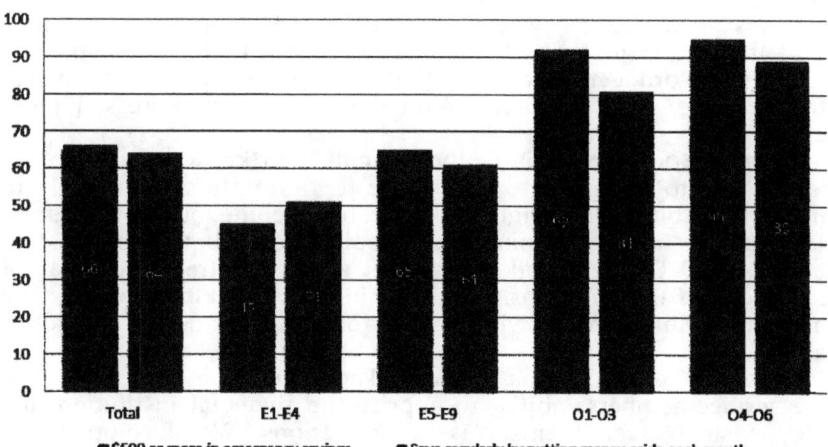

Savings Habits

Senator BOOZMAN. I think that would be really helpful, if—again, I am not saying that we are not doing a good job of that, and yet, I do think it is important to measure things.

Mrs. Petraeus, you mentioned the incident with the unscrupulous for-profit college recruiters in VA hospitals, and again, we can argue the appropriateness of that or not. I think if you go through the—so many members of the service, because they have a lot of leeway in how they get the education program benefits, a lot of for-profits, you know, many people have benefited from that. Yet, as you indicated earlier in your testimony, I guess my concern is why, if you have a situation like that, is the commanding officer not aware as to what can be done, maybe working with Mr. Halperin or Colonel Kantwill, to remedy that?

I mean, that is so cut-and-dried. I think that is a blatant thing that we simply should not be tolerating. One of the frustrations I have had a little bit, which I would like to broaden a little, is that sometimes it is really hard to figure out, not particularly this law, but protecting servicemembers and veterans in general.

It is really difficult to figure out which agency that we direct preditor complaints to so that they can go after them. But in this case, to me, it seems like we have got a little bit of a breakdown, perhaps Colonel Kantwill, Mrs. Petraeus, Mr. Halperin, in the sense that the commanders have the ability to know who can put the fear in whoever is doing that.

Ms. PETRAEUS. Well, I would mention that these are veterans, so they are no longer in the active duty military and they would not have a chain of command like that.

Senator BOOZMAN. But you have got somebody—you have got a chain of command in the hospital.

Ms. PETRAEUS. Yeah, and I think one concern has been, really, the lack of sort of a central complaint portal to actually report issues like this, and that has been addressed by the President in his Executive Order and Congress as well has looked at it. They are working hard to have one place to go where you can field these complaints. And we look forward to having that database up and running.

I was testifying last week with the folks from the VA and they said they hope to have that going by the fall. So, we hope that when the word gets out about that, that people will know where they can go with complaints and then they can addressed more effectively.

Senator BOOZMAN. It is really difficult, you know, if you do not know who to complain to and where to find enforcement. Talk to me a little bit about—right now we have come out with a short form as far as complaining. Do people know about that? Is that being used? Can you talk a little bit about the frequency that—I know one of the problems was that things were pretty complex. We have made that simpler with a short form. Can you talk a little bit about that?

Colonel KANTWILL. Yes, Senator. The short form relates more to the servicemembers' ability to apprise the financial institution that they wish to avail themselves of protections. We developed that form with our colleagues at the Financial Services Roundtable in the Housing Policy Council. It has been distributed to the force and it looks like it is working very, very well.

In short, it makes military orders, which can be very complicated and difficult to read, much easier to use by the financial institutions. So, that has helped. On the complaint front, sir, two of the biggest settlements that my colleagues have discussed were begun by individual servicemembers making complaints through legal assistance attorneys. So, we think we are doing very well in this regard as well.

Senator BOOZMAN. Good. That is excellent. Thank you, Mr. Chairman.

Chairman SANDERS. Thank you, Senator Boozman. Let me just thank the panel for their excellent work on this very, very important issue. We look forward to working with you all in the future. Thanks very much for being with us this morning.

I want to welcome Mr. Paul Leonard who is the Senior Vice President at the Housing Policy Council of the Financial Services Roundtable. I want to thank you very much for being with us today. Mr. Leonard, if you would like to begin, we would love to hear from you.

STATEMENT OF PAUL LEONARD, SENIOR VICE PRESIDENT, HOUSING POLICY COUNCIL, THE FINANCIAL SERVICES ROUNDTABLE

Mr. LEONARD. Thank you, Mr. Chairman and Senator Boozman, for holding this important hearing today. I am Paul Leonard, Senior Vice President of Government Affairs for the Housing Policy Council, which is part of the Financial Services Roundtable. Our members are the leading national mortgage finance companies.

Our President, John Dalton, was unable to testify today and sends his apologies to the Committee. Secretary Dalton served as the Secretary of the Navy for 5 years and has a strong personal interest in this issue. I know this is an important issue for the Chairman and Members of the Committee.

Our members are intensely focused on strengthening their ability to comply with the Servicemembers Civil Relief Act and to improve their customer service for military personnel, veterans, and their families. We appreciate the leadership of Colonel Kantwill, the Department of Defense, Mrs. Petraeus and the CFPB, and the Congress in this effort.

My testimony will focus on industry efforts to improve their SCRA compliance and other efforts to assist veterans and military personnel. On SCRA, our member companies are working diligently to fully comply with all elements of SCRA. While the SCRA requires that a servicemember notify their financial services company to activate certain benefits such as the 6 percent cap, lenders recognize they have responsibilities, liability, and reputational risks should they foreclose on a property, regardless of whether notification was provided.

As Congress considers expanding SCRA to cover new consumers, we also ask that you examine improving the Defense Manpower Data Center, the DMDC, to help ensure that benefits and protections can be applied in the most efficient manner possible.

On industry efforts to improve compliance with the SCRA, our members are expanding personnel, adding resources, improving communication and training across business lines to better serve military customers, for example, one company has added an additional 490 personnel focused solely on SCRA and military customer assistance.

Companies have created military advisory committees led by senior executives, often with a military background, to spearhead efforts to improve service to military customers. A joint resource that we have been using to help reach more military families is the

Hope Now Alliance, which is a voluntary industry, non-profit fore-closure prevention effort that works closely with Treasury on the Making Home Affordable program.

Hope Now now holds in-person outreach events to contact and assist the stressed homeowners on their mortgage problems. Hope Now is now holding outreach events for military families on or near military bases. Since 2011, Hope Now has conducted nine on-base military outreach events. There are two non-base events scheduled, one in San Antonio, TX, on August 17, and one in San Bernardino, CA, on August 24.

At these events, Hope Now also seeks to inform servicemembers about their SCRA protections. Anecdotally, according to exit surveys taken by Hope Now at military events, more than 80 percent of the active duty members who participated in an event were not aware of their SCRA protections. Obviously, those are families that are having difficulty.

At these events, personnel can also learn about their mortgage options and receive counseling from independent, non-profit agencies. At a recent event at Joint Base Lewis-McChord, a homeowner said they were very pleased with the outcome. They are going to be able to address their mortgage situation, and it met and exceeded their expectations.

Now, I mentioned that there are some weaknesses in the SCRA benefits notification process, and one is that military personnel often do not notify their financial services of their status. We recognize that servicemembers face many other challenges in their lives which may cause them not to notify their financial services company of their status. They are being called up, they are getting briefings on many other issues, and sometimes they just do not do it.

One of our member companies reports that out of their military customer base who are date-eligible for SCRA benefits, only 31 percent have submitted military orders to them to activate their benefits. So, we support alternatives to help improve the process for proactively identifying SCRA individuals.

We want to work with Congress and the Department of Defense to improve procedures for applying SCRA. As Colonel Kantwill mentioned in his discussion with Senator Boozman, in 2011 and 2012, our members worked with DOD to develop an active duty status short form to improve communication of active duty orders from servicemembers for their financial services company.

While it is improving, the penetration of the form is not as broad as we would like it to be, but it is an example of the cooperation between the industry and DOD. The DMDC has become a critical tool for the financial services industry to strengthen compliance with SCRA. Cooperation between industry and DOD is essential to enable DMDC to identify individuals who qualify for SCRA protections. We have worked with DOD on improvements to the DMDC system and we thank the Department for making these changes.

Additional improvements will be needed, particularly if Congress considers adding additional populations, because the database will have to be able to provide identification of spouses, disabled veterans, or other classes Congress may choose to designate.

In closing, I just want to note another joint effort by the Housing Policy Council and the Hope Now Alliance called Project Patriotism Homes for Veterans. Attached to my testimony is a white paper on industry efforts to transfer REO properties to veterans and military families. We believe that thousands of these homes will be transferred to deserving veterans and families in the coming years, and it is a good example of the industry and non-profit cooperation to assist military personnel, veterans, and their families.

Thank you for the opportunity to testify and I look forward to working with you and answering any questions.

[The prepared statement of Mr. Leonard follows:]

PREPARED STATEMENT OF PAUL M. LEONARD, SENIOR VICE PRESIDENT, GOVERNMENT AFFAIRS, HOUSING POLICY COUNCIL, FINANCIAL SERVICES ROUNDTABLE

Chairman Sanders, Ranking Member Burr and Members of the Committee thank you for holding this important hearing today focused on the unique financial services issues affecting Servicemembers and their families. We thank you for the invitation to participate.

My name is Paul Leonard and I am the Senior Vice President of Government Affairs for the Housing Policy Council (HPC) of The Financial Services Roundtable (FSR). The Housing Policy Council is part of The Financial Services Roundtable and our members are thirty-one of the leading national mortgage finance companies in America. HPC members originate, service and insure mortgages.

Since early 2011, the members of the Housing Policy Council and members of The Financial Services Roundtable, both individually and collectively, have been intensely focused on strengthening their ability to comply with the Servicemembers Civil Relief Act (SCRA) and in broadening and improving their customer service and support for military service personnel, veterans and their families.[1]

As part of this focused effort, HPC has worked closely with Colonel Paul Kantwill and his team at the Department of Defense (DOD); Mrs. Holly Petraeus and her team at the Consumer Financial Protection Bureau's (CFPB) Office of Servicemember Affairs; the Congress, and the industry to increase understanding of, and find solutions to, the unique financial challenges that Servicemembers and military families face. I want to thank Colonel Kantwill and Mrs. Petraeus for their leadership and for working closely with us on addressing these important issues.

The Housing Policy Council has a Servicemember Affairs working group and one of the key goals of this group is to improve compliance with the SCRA. My testimony today will focus on three important points about industry efforts to improve compliance with SCRA:

(1) Our members are working diligently to fully comply with all elements of SCRA and provide assistance to military customers on their financial needs;

(2) While elements of the statute, most notably the 6% interest rate cap, provides that the servicemember must notify their financial services company and submit official military orders for liability to be imposed, a servicemember's failure to notify does not remove the risk to the lender should it foreclose on a property when proper notification would have prevented that; and

(3) As Congress considers whether to expand SCRA to new consumer classes such as the spouse of a deceased servicemember killed while on active duty, we ask that consideration also be given to improving the ability of industry participants to better utilize the Defense Manpower Data Center (DMDC) at DOD to supplement the notification process with the goal of insuring that benefits and protections are applied to protected classes in the most timely and efficient manner possible.

(1) Industry efforts to comply with SCRA:

FSR and HPC member companies continue to expand their personnel and resources dedicated to serving their military customers. Many companies continue to hire military veterans, and in some cases their spouses, to staff customer service units as well as internal compliance and military liaison positions that are trained and certified in SCRA. Several of our companies have instituted specific programs and services to meet the financial needs of our men and women in uniform as well.

---

[1] See Project Patriotism Addendum, including the Financial Services Roundtable's survey of member companies and the various programs, products and services focused to military consumers, as part of this testimony.

Company efforts to improve communication, collaboration, compliance and training across business lines to better service military customer accounts, and to ensure protections such as SCRA have come a long way in the last several years. This progress has occurred with the leadership and cooperation of the Department of Defense, CFPB, the Department of Justice and the commitment of the companies that we work with at the Housing Policy Council and The Financial Services Roundtable.

One resource that has been utilized to help reach more military customers is the HOPE NOW Alliance, of which HPC is a founding member. HOPE NOW is a voluntary industry and non-profit foreclosure prevention and home preservation effort that works closely with the Treasury Department on the Making Home Affordable programs. HOPE NOW holds in-person outreach events and other efforts to contact distressed homeowners across the country and provide information and assistance to them on home retention and other mortgage workout options that are available to them.

HOPE NOW has expanded its outreach model to conduct outreach events for military families on and near military bases across the United States to the extent the Department of Defense permits it to do so. The on-base meetings permit mortgage servicers and non-profit counselors to reach more service men and women and educate them on workout options available to them in situations such as when their loans are underwater or when they face a Permanent Change of Station. In addition, the HOPE NOW events also help to improve servicemembers' awareness of their SCRA protections. According to exit surveys taken by HOPE NOW at military outreach events since 2011, more than 80% of active-duty members of the military who participated in a HOPE NOW sponsored event were not aware of their protections under SCRA and had not taken any action to activate the protections. In other words, for many servicemembers, they learned about their SCRA protections for the first time when they sat down, face to face with their lender to discuss options on their mortgage situation.

There is a real need to continue efforts to educate military personnel about the SCRA protections that are available to them and that they understand the process to activate the protections. The HOPE NOW Alliance is continuing military outreach events and will be in two military markets in August, one in San Antonio Texas on August 17 and a second in San Bernardino California on August 24. We want to continue and work with all other stakeholders to improve education on SCRA and to better serve our men and women in uniform.

(2) Weaknesses in the notification process for SCRA benefits:

In practice, the process to initiate SCRA benefits and protections often fails because the servicemember does not provide notification of their active-duty status to their financial services company. The industry recognizes that there are a number of challenges that a servicemember faces which may prevent timely submission of military orders or other documentation to their financial service provider. The industry supports exploring alternatives to help improve the process for identifying and providing benefits to SCRA eligible individuals.

We want to work with Congress, the Department of Defense and other stakeholders to develop new tools and improve current processes and procedures for applying SCRA protections. In 2011 industry, working cooperatively with DOD, developed an ''Active Duty Status'' short form designed to improve communication of active duty orders from servicemembers to their financial services company. The form was approved by DOD and implementation began in January 2012. Although the use of the form is not yet as broad as we would like, it is an example of cooperative work between key stakeholders to improve the SCRA notification process and enhance compliance capabilities by the industry. We want to expand the use of the ''Active Duty Status'' short form and are prepared to work with key stakeholders to improve its use as an additional tool for compliance with the law. We are also exploring ideas with our member companies through our Servicemember Affairs working group to develop new tools to enhance compliance with SCRA.

(3) Defense Manpower Data Center Data base (DMDC):

The Defense Manpower Data Center has become the primary tool used by the financial services industry for strengthening compliance with SCRA. The use of the DMDC system has been recognized by Federal and state regulators such as the OCC and the Department of Justice in various agreements as an important tool to enhance compliance with SCRA. Since the DMDC was designed for other purposes separate from its use as a SCRA verification tool, cooperation between the industry and the Department of Defense is essential to enable its effective use in identifying servicemembers and other individuals who qualify for SCRA protections. We continue to work closely with DOD to suggest enhancements and improvements to the

DMDC system that have improved the efficiency of the database. DMDC has made improvements to the system in the last year that our members have welcomed as positive enhancements, and we thank the Department of Defense for making those adaptations.

There remains much to do to improve the system. These improvements are especially needed as Congress considers expanding SCRA protections to new consumer classes. The database needs additional changes and capabilities to enable it to provide identification of spouses, disabled veterans or other classes Congress may designate.

Many of the ongoing data integrity and data accuracy issues are documented in a report to Congress titled "Accuracy of Data in the Defense Enrollment Eligibility Reporting System (DEERS)," [2] which was required by section 595 of the National Defense Authorization Act for Fiscal Year 2013. Specific issues that our member companies continue to encounter with DMDC include:

• Unreliable data associated with National Guard and Reservists, particularly those individuals with Title 32 orders for state duty that transition to Title 10 status for Federal duty. From a compliance perspective, it can be challenging to capture date-eligible benefits of a servicemember that routinely changes status.

• Use of unique identifiers when retrieving data from DMDC.
   – For example, the system requires both a surname and SSN. This can lead to false negatives (which leads banks, creditors and other users to falsely believe that the person of interest in not a member of the military). This error often occurs when a servicemember has changed his or her last name, such as in the case of marriage, or where the DOD's record of the servicemember's surname differs from other official records. We believe that such errors would be eliminated if the system required only a valid SSN/Tax ID identifier.

We recognize Congressional interest in expanding SCRA to new consumer classes, but we urge that Congress consider enhancing the DMDC database system to provide accurate and reliable access to data that would enable the timely identification of new categories of individuals protected under the law. We invite Members of Congress to work with all key stakeholders here today to help improve the data integrity and accuracy of the DMDC system and identify the appropriate methods to achieve this goal.

One final note I would like to make in closing today is about a joint effort by the Housing Policy Council and the HOPE NOW Alliance on what we call our Project Patriotism Homes for Veterans initiative. In June of this year HPC issued a white paper on industry efforts to transition refurbished Real-Estate Owned or distressed properties to veterans, wounded warriors and military families. Our findings indicate that over the coming years thousands of these homes will have been transferred to deserving patriots and their families. A top recommendation from the paper was to convene a "Homes for Veterans" summit with key stakeholders engaged in this space, which we did last week. There are a number of actionable next steps we have taken from that summit that we believe can better enhance these Homes for Veterans programs, inter-connect stakeholders in this space, and enhance these models to a larger, more national scale. This initiative by the industry, in partnership with non-profits and third party groups, is a great example of ongoing efforts by the financial services industry to address the unique needs of the U.S. military and veteran populations.

I thank the Committee for the opportunity to testify today and look forward to working with you to address the unique financial services issues affecting servicemembers, veterans and military families.

―――――

RESPONSE TO POSTHEARING QUESTIONS SUBMITTED BY HON. JOHN D. ROCKEFELLER IV TO PAUL LEONARD, FINANCIAL SERVICES ROUNDTABLE

Question 1. There has been significant confusion over time related to one very important aspect of the SCRA: whether servicemembers are required to notify their lenders in order to be eligible for the protections it provides. You mentioned in your testimony that in the case of one of your member companies, only 31 percent of eligible servicemembers have notified their lender of their eligibility for SCRA protections. However, as you probably know, lenders only have to be affirmatively notified of a desire for an interest rate reduction—not of the entitlement of a servicemember to protection from foreclosure while they are on active duty status. That being said,

―――――

[2] Accuracy of Data in the Defense Enrollment Eligibility Reporting System Plan, March 2013, p. 5.

some banks have argued in court that servicemembers were not protected from fore-closure under the SCRA because they did not provide the bank with notice. What is the Financial Services Roundtable's current understanding of the obligations of servicemembers to notify their lenders that they are protected under this important law?

Response. For the foreclosure protection, under SCRA law, servicemembers are not required to notify their lender. For the 6% interest rate cap benefit, service-members are required to contact their lender. With that said, many of the protec-tions under SCRA, including protection from foreclosure, have specific eligibility pe-riods that extend beyond the period of a protected individuals active duty end date. The only method by which financial services companies can verify when a service-member's protection from foreclosure begins and ends under SCRA is through offi-cial military orders and/or a positive identification of military service through the Defense Manpower Data Center (DMDC). Beyond those two means a company is ex-tremely limited in their ability to effectively verify and apply protections within the legislatively mandated period of time. Furthermore, NSS standards created required foreclosure protections above and beyond the SCRA law (e.g. deployed internation-ally to a hazardous duty area) and these cases can only be determined by the ser-vicemember submitting official orders or military documentation.

RESPONSE TO POSTHEARING QUESTIONS SUBMITTED BY HON. MARK BEGICH TO FINANCIAL SERVICES ROUNDTABLE

Question 5. You mentioned two initiatives, Hope Now events and Project Patriot-ism Homes, what are some other initiatives the industry has taken to improve serv-ice to military customers?

Response. Our member companies continue to offer pre-service and post-service financial education programs to military customers if they wish to utilize them. As mentioned in our testimony, many of our companies have expanded their operations to better serve military customers including adding single points of contact for the life of loans and multiple companies actively participate in programs focused on hir-ing veterans and their spouses.

As part of Project Patriotism, we conducted a survey of members to both the Roundtable and the Housing Policy Council on programs, products and services they provide to military customers, veterans and military families. More than 1/3rd of our companies participated in the survey. Here are some of those results:

• Overall, the vast majority of survey respondents provide employment outreach for active military, military families, and veterans.
• 50% provide job training for veterans.
• 50% provide special financial service products for active military.
• About 1/3rd of respondents provide financial literacy for active military, mili-tary families and veterans.
• The majority of respondents provide special programs and outreach efforts for active military, military families, or veterans.
• Over 50% of respondents provide special services to help active-duty Service-members re-acclimate to civilian life.

Question 6. How does the industry currently utilize DMDC, how important is it to compliance, and what other tools exist for purposes of SCRA compliance?

Response. The Defense Manpower Data Center has become the primary tool used by the financial services industry for strengthening compliance with SCRA. In prac-tice, the process to initiate SCRA benefits and protections, particularly the interest rate cap benefit, often fails because the servicemember does not provide notification of their active-duty status to their financial services company, and the data in DMDC is at times inaccurate or inconsistent for the timely application of providing foreclosure protections. The industry recognizes that there are a number of chal-lenges that a servicemember faces which may prevent timely submission of military orders or other documentation to their financial services provider. The industry sup-ports exploring alternatives to help improve the process for identifying and pro-viding benefits and protections to SCRA eligible individuals. For example:

• We worked closely with DOD to create a new tool for compliance in the Active Duty Status short form. The form was designed to improve communication of active duty orders from servicemembers to their financial services company.
• Through the FSR-HPC Servicemember Affairs working group we are actively exploring new ideas to improve industry compliance and welcome all stakeholders and their ideas on this initiative.

Generally speaking, member servicers have implemented significant controls to ensure that all customers are evaluated for SCRA protection throughout the default servicing lifecycle. For example, many member servicers are checking the DMDC prior to referring a customer to foreclosure, checking again prior to default judgment, checking again prior to foreclosure sale, checking immediately after the foreclosure sale, and checking again prior to eviction. These proactive efforts to check customers with known and unknown military status have greatly improved the servicers' ability to detect qualifying individuals and apply the protections afforded under the Act.

RESPONSE TO POSTHEARING QUESTIONS SUBMITTED BY HON. RICHARD BLUMENTHAL TO FINANCIAL SERVICES ROUNDTABLE

Question 2. Mr. Leonard, thank you for your tireless work on behalf of our country's veterans, servicemembers, and their families. Can you elaborate on the harm that you have seen caused by the long-term financial products not covered under the Military Lending Act? I've called upon the Department of Defense to update their guidelines for this act to cover predatory lenders who use open-ended products to charge high APRs to veterans-some as high as 400%. Could you talk about any cases you have seen of the harm that high APRs—such as the open-ended products offered to servicemembers at APRs as high as 400%—can cause to servicemembers?

Response. As our testimony notes, the Housing Policy Council has primarily focused on improving industry compliance with the Servicemembers Civil Relief Act (SCRA). We have not focused on the Military Lending Act. We do believe that it is beneficial for military personnel and the financial services industry to improve and strengthen financial education for servicemembers at all phases of their career since financial education plays a critical role in helping servicemembers and their families use credit products wisely.

RESPONSE TO POSTHEARING QUESTIONS SUBMITTED BY HON. MAZIE HIRONO TO FINANCIAL SERVICES ROUNDTABLE

Question 3. After implementing the suggestions you listed, do you think the Defense Manpower Data Center (DMDC) system is at the point where there should be no more incidents of SCRA violations?

Response. We believe that the enhancements by DOD to DMDC have improved the system, including the ability to process batches of accounts through the system to verify military service of a company's portfolio of customers. The industry has improved their compliance capabilities with SCRA, as was noted in the testimony of Mrs. Petreaus of CFPB and Colonel Kantwill of DOD at the hearing on July 31. As our testimony notes, we continue to experience a severe gap in submission of a written notice and official military orders to companies in activating the 6% interest rate cap benefit. If the DMDC data was inclusive for all servicemembers, (e.g. full time military, reserve, guardsmen, early alert notification, servicemembers on classified orders etc.); and also was accurate and timely, the industry could greatly improve compliance with the SCRA's foreclosure protection component. Furthermore, if the industry could utilize data from the DMDC to activate the 6% interest rate cap benefit, this would greatly improve the process and servicemembers' experience (servicemembers would not need to submit orders). With these enhancements and some level of statutory protection or safe harbor for those financial services companies that utilize and rely on the DMDC to provide SCRA benefits and protections to servicemembers, the industry would be able to further improve compliance. The ongoing data integrity issues related to DMDC, however, prevents full compliance with the law. Questions remain as to whether active-duty personnel are even familiar with SCRA, the protections they are entitled to, and how to activate these protections. There remain a number of challenges that need to be addressed to better enhance the industry's ability to comply with SCRA, including improving education to servicemembers on their rights and protections under the law.

Question 4. Your testimony indicates that the DMDC is still being improved. Are further changes necessary to run an accurate search engine that provides current records of individuals' active-duty/deployment periods?

Response. Yes, we do believe additional changes can and should be made to improve the system and the ability to retrieve data from DMDC. For example, as mentioned in our testimony, the ability to search the system utilizing a social security number as the primary search field would reduce false-negatives from the database. Because data is manually input by DOD and the military services, and queries through the system are driven through multiple fields such as the last name, the odds of a false-negative are high. Indications are that DOD is working to automate many internal processes to improve data accuracy and the ability to retrieve such data more rapidly; however, it is unclear where that process stands. Additionally, as Congress considers expanding SCRA to new consumer classes such as the surviving spouse to a deceased active-duty servicemember, access to the appropriate data from DMDC would provide an additional verification tool for the purposes of compliance with any new requirements under the law.

Chairman SANDERS. Thank you very much, Mr. Leonard. Mr. Leonard, let me begin by asking you this. In a 2012 report, the Government Accountability Office identified over 14,000 instances of financial institutions failing to properly reduce servicemembers' mortgage interest rates and over 300 improper foreclosures. How did this happen?

Mr. LEONARD. Senator, as was documented by the previous witnesses, there were shortcomings across the industry, I think, throughout the crisis from 2007. Now we are coming out of it, but I think many financial service companies were overwhelmed by the number of consumers in distress. I think there were—I do think that companies did not have integrated systems to identify military personnel promptly.

As I said, oftentimes the covered individuals do not identify proactively, so the companies need to do it. That is one reason since 2011 we have been working with DOD on making the DMDC more useful in proactively identifying, so we do not have to rely on—put the burden on the servicemember.

Chairman SANDERS. Do you anticipate that there will be a reduction in these types of occurrences?

Mr. LEONARD. I think there already has been a reduction. If you look at the agreements, I think since companies—these problems were called to their attention beginning in 2010, 2011. As I said, our member companies have dedicated tremendous amounts of resources, hired new staff often with a military background, and also integrated product lines so that they know if there is an SCRA issue in mortgage. They are going to find out if that also applies to credit cards or auto loans. So, I think there has been a dramatic improvement and effort over the last several years.

Chairman SANDERS. So, what I am hearing you say is you do not anticipate the kind of problems that we have seen in the past?

Mr. LEONARD. I can tell you that our companies, the major national and regional companies, are very focused on this issue. They are doing everything they can to make sure that mistakes or problems do not occur again.

Chairman SANDERS. I am glad to hear that.

Senator Boozman.

Senator BOOZMAN. Thank you, Mr. Chairman. I think one of the ways that we can do that, Mr. Chairman, is to make it such that—the statistic you gave—that 80 percent essentially are not aware of their rights with the law. Am I correct?

Mr. LEONARD. Yes. And that was——

Senator BOOZMAN. That you surveyed. And that is not an official survey perhaps, or whatever, but a pretty good indicator that there is a problem. But I think as we do a better job in telling our servicemembers—and I think particularly our commanding officers because that is where you go to when you are having a problem——

making sure that they understand and that there is, you know, how you go about doing that, I think, is really important and really will be our best bet for eliminating problems in the future or, you know, dealing with these companies that are being unscrupulous.

Tell me about the short form and the long form. Now, the long form, does the short form replace that?

Mr. LEONARD. The short form is intended to replace—you know, as you know, orders are many pages and very detailed.

Senator BOOZMAN. Right.

Mr. LEONARD. But the key thing to initiate benefits is the dates of active duty service. So, the short form has the key information that the financial service company needs to initiate benefits and make sure that they are applied when the servicemember is entitled to it. So, the short form is one method to try to speed up the process so there is no gap in that servicemember getting their benefits.

The other method we would like to see is—what our companies do is they go to the Defense Manpower Data Center, they run their customer base against the database, and find out who is on active duty. Now, we recognize that there are—DMDC is used for a variety of other purposes by the Department. It is not just for identifying SCRA benefits, but that has become a very important role for it.

So, we would like to work with the Department and the Congress to make additional improvements. For example, in a secure manner, using a Social Security number to identify the covered individual, because often the names can be slightly different. If it is a maiden name or hyphenated name, it may come back as a false negative.

The major companies, the national companies, we are talking about tens of thousands of files that they need to check against the database. But as you said, we think the Department, with the help of CFPB, is very focused on the financial education part of it. Our members are focused on it, both individually through outreach, and the addendum to our testimony talks about some of the individual efforts companies have made on financial education with their military customers.

Senator BOOZMAN. Can you follow up on that? Because, I guess, my final question would be, you know, people are working very, very hard on this issue and we have got a good law in place. What else do we need to do? Can you give some examples of what—you know, you said—give some examples there and then again, where else do we need to focus?

Mr. LEONARD. I think what we are seeing is that the efforts that the Department has underway with the advice of CFPB on financial education, as you noted, it is very important to have the buy-in of the commanding officer, that he or she identifies it as a priority. For example, at the recent outreach event that Hope Now had at Joint Base Lewis-McChord in Washington, the CO said, ''This is something we should do. We should have this event so that both military and base civilian personnel and veterans could come in and talk with either a non-profit counselor or their financial services provider.''

I think our companies and the industry in general is getting more focused on it and I think some of the material we provided in the testimony shows that there is an increased attention, that this is a unique consumer segment. As Chairman Sanders said at the beginning of the hearing, they have got a lot going on in their lives, even much—you know, other families have a lot of stresses, but military families have probably the most stress.

So, that is one reason why we think enabling companies in a secure manner to use the database more effectively, to say, OK, we have identified this person, they should be getting the coverage from the State.

Senator BOOZMAN. OK. Thank you, Mr. Chairman.

Chairman SANDERS. John, if I could, I would like to ask another question. I understand that the financial industry is involved in an initiative, Project Patriotism Homes for Veterans. Homelessness among veterans has been a very serious problem in this country for decades. I think in recent years, we have begun to maybe make a little bit of progress in that area. Can you explain to us what the financial industry intends to do to help the VA and all of us address the problem of veterans' homelessness?

Mr. LEONARD. Well, Mr. Chairman, this particular effort is focused on—as you know, one of the effects of the financial crisis was that there was an increasing amount of distressed properties that were foreclosed on. Many of them were vacant and in disrepair. And a number of our companies and non-profits started asking, "Well, could we use some of these REO properties to provide homes for veterans and military personnel?"

So, companies individually began working with non-profits to figure out how could they identify potential REO properties that could be transferred to the non-profit and the non-profit could identify veterans and servicemembers who would be able to take over the home, either in a straight donation, some type of sweat equity, or a reduced mortgage?

And that is what the Project Patriotism paper is about. It is to document the different efforts that are underway.

Chairman SANDERS. What kind of numbers are we talking about? How many homes have been transferred?

Mr. LEONARD. In the last year, I think there were 500 homes, but we expect that to climb into the thousands. The problem is, is that there are a number of factors involved. You have to find a home in an area where a veteran wants to live.

Chairman SANDERS. I do understand the complexity of it, but at this point, you are saying there were about 500 vacant homes and now they are occupied by veterans and their families?

Mr. LEONARD. Yes.

Chairman SANDERS. And you expect that number to continue?

Mr. LEONARD. Yes, and we can provide the Committee with an update on the number.

Chairman SANDERS. I would love to see that. And is this project taking place across the country?

Mr. LEONARD. Yes. Most of our members and major national lenders are involved and they work with different non-profits. In the paper, it documents the types of non-profits. Each of the non-profits may have a slightly different approach, either straight donation or sweat equity.

Chairman SANDERS. So, it is going from the bank to the non-profit to the veteran?

Mr. LEONARD. Exactly. The bank provides the property and some of the funding, but the selection of the veteran and working with them to make sure that they can be a successful homeowner is done through the non-profit so that they understand specifics: does the veteran need to be near medical facilities; are they going to be near family; and that type of thing.

Chairman SANDERS. Please get as much information on that effort as you can to my staff. I would be appreciative.

[This information was received and is being held in Committee files.]

Senator Boozman.

Senator BOOZMAN. Thank you, Mr. Chairman. Again, we appreciate your efforts and we really look forward to working with you. Hopefully you can help us strengthen things; then, as importantly, help us in providing the outreach.

I think that is really what we lack more than anything, is just making the servicemember aware of the significant protections that they have. And right now, that seems to be a challenge which is just going to take everyone working together to do a better job on that. So, thank you for being here.

Mr. LEONARD. Thank you, Senator. Thank you, Mr. Chairman.

Chairman SANDERS. Mr. Leonard, thank you very much. With that, this hearing is adjourned.

[Whereupon, at 10:48 a.m., the hearing was adjourned.]